Europe and the Atlantic Relationship

Europe and the Atlantic Relationship

Issues of Identity, Security and Power

Edited by

Douglas Eden
Head of the Centre for Study of International Affairs (Europe and America)
Middlesex University

First published in Great Britain 2000 by
MACMILLAN PRESS LTD
Houndmills, Basingstoke, Hampshire RG21 6XS and London
Companies and representatives throughout the world

A catalogue record for this book is available from the British Library.

ISBN 0–333–75345–3

 First published in the United States of America 2000 by
ST. MARTIN'S PRESS, INC.,
Scholarly and Reference Division,
175 Fifth Avenue, New York, N.Y. 10010

ISBN 0–312–23408–2

Library of Congress Cataloging-in-Publication Data
Europe and the Atlantic relationship : issues of identity, security, and power / edited by Douglas Eden.
p.   cm.
Includes bibliographical references and index.
ISBN 0–312–23408–2 (cloth)
1. North Atlantic Treaty Organization. 2. European Union. 3. Europe–
–Relations—North America. 4. North America—Relations—Europe. 5. European
cooperation. 6. European federation. I. Eden, Douglas.

UA646.3 .E789   2000
355'.031090821 — dc21

00–023340

This book is printed on paper suitable for recycling and made from fully managed and sustained forest sources.

10   9   8   7   6   5   4   3   2   1
09   08   07   06   05   04   03   02   01   00

Printed and bound in Great Britain by
Antony Rowe Ltd, Chippenham, Wiltshire

Contents

Preface vi

Notes on the Contributors xiv

1   NATO and the Atlantic Relationship 1
    Douglas Eden

2   NATO's Enlargement: Limited, Controversial, Inevitable 13
    William Mader

3   The Future of NATO and the Transatlantic Alliance in the
    Twenty-First Century 30
    Geoffrey Lee Williams

4   The American Policy Debate on NATO Enlargement 57
    William Schneider, Jr

5   The Strategic Environment: the Next Twenty Years' Crisis? 71
    Alan Lee Williams

6   Development of the Atlantic Relationship: a View from
    the British Foreign and Commonwealth Office 82
    P.J. Priestley

7   The Politics of Trade in an Ever-Closer Community 92
    Don E. Newquist

8   Trade Developments in the Western Hemisphere:
    Implications for Transatlantic Relations 101
    Joseph A. McKinney

9   'Euroland' vs 'Big Europe': EMU, Transatlantic Relations and
    the Eastern Enlargements of NATO and the European Union 117
    Martin J. Dedman

10 The Transatlantic Implications of European Monetary
    Union 132
    Martin Holmes

Index 153

Preface: the State of Transatlantic Relations

In recent years, deep-seated conflicts of interest and perception have appeared among the European and North American members of the Atlantic Community. Such conflicts were suppressed during the Cold War in the interest of alliance unity against a common threat. In the 1990s, there has been a greater inclination to pursue differences, although open confrontation is normally avoided and the real interests at stake are rarely stated clearly for public debate.

The recent conflicts have been couched or concealed in positioning and rhetoric over development of the Community's two greatest institutions, the European Union (EU) and the North Atlantic Treaty Organisation (NATO). More particularly, the development at issue concerns enlargement of the two to include more members, the deeper integration of the EU and the reorganisation of NATO's structure and mission to meet its members' needs in the post-Cold War world. Should either or both NATO and the EU be enlarged, and if both, in what order? How far should the European Union integrate and merge the sovereignties of its member states? If both integration and enlargement of the Union take place, should the two processes occur simultaneously, or should one process have priority over the other?

Should the Europeans bear a greater share of NATO's burden? Can they afford to? Can or should the European Union develop a Common Foreign and Security Policy (CFSP) to pursue a European Security and Defence Identity (ESDI) within the NATO alliance? Are such a policy and identity feasible and would they bring Europe more into partnership or conflict with the United States and Canada? To what extent would the United States support and subsidise these developments? How will they fit in with NATO's new 'Strategic Concept' of a wider peacemaking and peacekeeping doctrine using Combined Joint Task Forces (CJTF) and cooperating with non-members of NATO who are official partners of the alliance (Partnership for Peace – PfP)? How will the change in NATO's mission and military doctrine affect relations with Russia?

Can the new NATO and the new ESDI meet the requirements of their citizens' regional and global interests, or will parochialism and nationalism or self-serving protectionism by governing elites limit their success? Will European Economic and Monetary Union (EMU) be used to limit or curtail American access to European markets, including defence procurement? Will resentment or fear of American technological leadership, both military and commercial, dominate European councils and lead to estrangement and the decline of the transatlantic relationship? If the United States finds itself discriminated against in trade by its European allies, will it retaliate only commercially or will the strength of its public opinion be turned against continuing America's guarantee of Europe's stability and security?

These are widely significant security, economic, commercial and cultural questions for the whole Atlantic Community, not military questions alone for the alliance or monetary and constitutional questions alone for the EU. Security policy and relations cannot be unaffected by disputes, conflict and retaliation over trade policy. If American logistic and diplomatic support is needed to sustain a more independent and united EU foreign policy, it may not be forthcoming if EU economic policy seeks to limit or exclude US access to European markets. If European cooperation is needed to share the burden of reviving the world economy, it may not be forthcoming if US global policy disregards European interests or if the North American Free Trade Agreement (NAFTA) discriminates against EU access to Western hemisphere markets.

This book seeks to explore all these questions. It addresses the current state of the transatlantic relationship and prospects for the development of the Atlantic Community in the light of recent events. It looks into the future to consider the threats and options that face the Community in the twenty-first century.

The last year of the twentieth, 1999, will be recorded as a milestone in the history of transatlantic relations. The principal institution of the relationship, the North Atlantic Treaty Organisation, expanded to the East for the first time since the reunification of Germany, and shortly afterward undertook its first belligerent military action. Eleven members of the European Union adopted the euro in place of their national currencies and as a major trading currency alongside the US dollar. Meanwhile, the world's most significant economic partners, the United States and the European Union, contemplated a trade war for the first time since the Second World War.

Poland, Hungary and the Czech Republic joined the NATO alliance in March. Within a few days, NATO was at war for the first time in its 50-year history, launching Operation Allied Force against Slobodan Milosevic's Yugoslav state. In the midst of war, in April, the leaders of the 19 NATO member countries met in Washington to celebrate the alliance's

50th anniversary and to declare a new 'Strategic Concept' doctrine. NATO was transformed from a purely defensive alliance, which would react only if one of its members were attacked, to a policing and peace-keeping alliance, prepared to initiate or support pre-emptive or defensive action beyond its members' borders in defence of common vital interests. In defence of democracy and shared values and interests, NATO's alliance of democracies adopted a more or less traditional forward policy, previously more characteristic of multinational imperial powers.

The first enactment of the new doctrine, the war over Kosovo, occurred before its formal adoption. It was successful in achieving its ultimately stated objective: the restoration of the Kosovo Albanians to their lands and homes. No less significantly, it forced many NATO members to face realities they had previously avoided and may have helped to engender a clearer understanding and appreciation of the Atlantic relationship.

Germany rejoined the international system as a great power, her SPD/ Green government coalition providing the leadership that committed her to active participation in the war and the enforcement of the peace. France discovered the political and military cost of years of antagonism to American leadership of the alliance, her leaders committing her to a major presence in the conflict in recognition of France's best interests, but discovering they lacked the equipment and technology to make an appropriate contribution. Yet, they stood firm for the alliance despite a startled and unsympathetic public conditioned by years of Gaullist rhetoric.

Britain, having made more of an investment in her forces, found she could make a contribution second only to the United States, despite deploying fewer aircraft than the French, and thus enjoy great influence. Italian leaders found, characteristically, that they could successfully reassure their allies of their commitment privately while reassuring their people of their dissent from their allies in public. The United States discovered that, if they exerted leadership, it would be accepted by their 18 allies; and that some of their allies were prepared to provide leadership or encouragement if Americans were uncertain. The fact that an apparently unwieldy alliance of 19 democracies maintained unity throughout the three months of the conflict was as great a boost for NATO as it was an unexpected disaster for Slobodan Milosevic.

In the ultimate NATO plan to use ground forces, which brought Milosevic's surrender, it is highly significant that the Europeans offered to bear the largest share of the fighting, the British and the French in particular volunteering almost their entire available national forces.

All of this augured well for another important event of 1999, the decision to develop a European Security and Defence Identity (ESDI) within NATO and a Common Foreign and Security Policy (CFSP) within the EU, both with American assistance. However, the Kosovo war demonstrated how hugely European defence expenditure would have to be increased to take full advantage of American technology, let alone achieve European self-sufficiency.

Another reminder in 1999 of Europe's inadequate defence technology was the dissemination by the United States to its allies of alarming information about the proliferation of ballistic missiles and weapons of mass destruction (WMD) among 'rogue' states, posing serious threats to both Europe and North America. As the development of anti-ballistic missile technology came to appear the most appropriate response to the threat, Britain and Germany indicated their willingness to contribute to an American ABM initiative. The events of 1999 proved again how essential it is to Europe's security and stability that the United States remains a fully committed European power.

Britain's effort to show herself a good European, hoping to increase her influence in the European Union, is most realistic when she offers to allocate her military strength to EU purposes. She is unable to exert much direct influence on the EU's economic policies as she is dwarfed by the German economy and outflanked by the special Franco-German relationship. In 1999, the British government was concerned that the introduction of the euro without Britain's participation should not diminish her influence even further. Hence, the British Prime Minister's offer at St Malo to cooperate with France and Germany to build the ESDI was a significant move to mobilise Britain's best card to gain French and German cooperation in areas of British national interest.

However, Britain's attempt to draw closer to her European allies while maintaining a close relationship with the United States is bedevilled by Continental and particularly French ambivalence toward the American connection. Here again the Kosovo experience was extremely helpful. Nevertheless, French – and thus, inevitably, German – attitudes toward trade questions in particular indicate a troublesome phenomenon in the Euro-American relationship.

It is appropriate at this point to say something about Germany's attachment to her special relationship with France. For 20 years until 1989, German governments had two overriding strategic concerns: to reassure Germany's neighbours and herself that she had rid herself of her ruinous nationalism and to achieve reunification. To succeed in the first objective, Germany needed to think 'European' at all times. Her leaders and commentators eschewed talk of German national interests. These were always termed 'European' interests. No members of the EU embraced Europeanism and European unity as fervently as the Germans. Any policy that suited them was fostered because it was 'good for Europe'. That it was good for Europe was proven if France approved. The wartime violation of Marianne produced a German war guilt that could only be expiated by French friendship and approval. However, while the Soviet threat loomed, Germany relied on American friendship for recognition of her new democratic credentials, for her security and for the key to national reunification. With the iron curtain's collapse in 1989 and the achievement of reunification in 1991, German priorities in friendship were subtly altered to place France ahead of America.

Throughout the Cold War, European security and politics were largely dominated by 'the German Question'. That has now been replaced, in part, by 'the European Question'. That is, will the new Europe of the EU turn inward against its Atlantic connections and establish a protectionist, statist and combative posture as much against North America as against China or Russia; or will it develop liberally in partnership with its North American allies? Recent rejection of proposals for a New Transatlantic Marketplace by France, and European Union breaches of the rules of the World Trade Organisation (WTO) to protect European interests against external competition, particularly from the United States, have raised alarms about the direction of EU policy. Popular anxieties (for example, over hormone-fed beef, genetically modified foods and protecting the banana crops of former colonies) have been carefully nurtured by European elites to build public support for protectionist policies, subtly promoting their own power by encouraging anti-Americanist sentiments. WTO findings against the EU's protectionist measures have been brusquely rejected by Brussels acting in accord with Franco-German policy and against British preferences. We have yet to see the consequences for the transatlantic relationship of American retaliation under WTO rules.

There are also fears that the newly introduced euro will be manipulated and the associated Stability Pact will be twisted or breached and stiff harmonisation taxes will be imposed to avoid necessary economic and welfare reforms; thus distorting the Single European Market and leading to an increasingly protectionist regime that commits further breaches of world trade agreements.

Are these fears overstated? Is the European economy about to revive and put all these anxieties to rest under a flood of prosperity and job creation, giving Europe's leaders the courage to liberalise and deregulate? The authors who have written chapters on trade and economics for this book rely on evidence of performance thus far to draw their conclusions.

The concerns of some security specialists about EU commercial policy, however, are reinforced by some of the national attitudes observed toward sharing the political and financial burden of collective defence under NATO. At a time when greater European commitment to defence expenditure is required to meet the requirements of ESDI and CFSP, Germany, for example, has announced intentions to cut defence spending by some $2.5 billion. There is also concern about the attitudes of some Europeans toward cooperation with North American allies over security policy outside the primary Treaty area. The French attitude toward Anglo-American policy in Iraq is a case in point. The reluctant quality of the support given by some allies to the alliance action in Kosovo is another.

This book is the second volume of contributions made at the annual Trent Park Conferences on 'The Future of the Atlantic Community', organised by the Centre for the Study of International Affairs (Europe and America) at Middlesex University, London. Four such conferences have now been held with the collaboration of the Atlantic Council of the United Kingdom and Baylor University.

The opening chapter of this book attempts to provide an informative and scene-setting overview of the current problems, concerns and hopes touched on above. The reader should find it a useful introduction to this very complicated subject, particularly in its efforts to explain the evolution of NATO doctrine and to relate security and economic/commercial matters to each other and the larger political questions. It also discusses the significance of the Kosovo war for NATO and the transatlantic relationship. William Mader then provides a more detailed description of the issues involved in NATO enlargement, including the concerns of Central and Eastern Europe. Geoffrey Lee Williams follows with an original and stimulating discussion of the forces shaping the future of the transatlantic alliance.

William Schneider Jr describes the American policy debate on NATO enlargement, explains American security interests in Europe and describes some of the threats, including ballistic missile and WMD proliferation, that must be faced. Alan Lee Williams surveys the strategic environment and warns that inadequate investment, cooperation and preparation of the NATO allies for the security challenges of the future risks incurring a 20 years' crisis to set beside the 1920s and 1930s. Philip Priestley portrays the official view of the New Labour government in

Britain on the development of the Atlantic relationship. His contribution has not been updated to take account of the Kosovo war. Don E. Newquist relates the course of EU–US trade relations in the light of the debates over NATO and EU expansion. Joseph A. McKinney reports on the effect of recent trade and regional developments in the Western hemisphere on transatlantic relations. Martin Dedman considers the effect of European Union development on the Atlantic relationship, including questions of enlargement and integration. Finally, Martin Holmes concentrates on the implications for the Atlantic relationship of European Economic and Monetary Union.

All of the contributions were either written directly for this book or are recently (1999) updated, revised and edited versions of papers presented at the Trent Park Conference of 1997. All of them develop strategic rather than short-term perspectives. With the partial exception of Philip Priestley's contribution, the contributors' observations and conclusions are either reinforced or not affected by the Kosovo war of March to June 1999. The first chapter in particular takes the strategic significance of the Balkan crisis, including the Kosovo war, fully into account.

The discussion cannot end here. This is an unfolding and evolving story. It remains the purpose of the Centre to continue monitoring and interpreting its course. The promise made in our previous volume has thus far been fulfilled. We plan to publish expanded, updated and revised contributions from the third and fourth annual Trent Park Conferences on the Future of the Atlantic Community, held in 1998 and 1999. As ever, I am grateful to all the conference participants and particularly to the contributors and the members of the Centre's Advisory Board for their cooperation and demonstration of transatlantic community.

DOUGLAS EDEN
Centre for Study of International Affairs
(Europe and America), Middlesex University,
London, July 1999

The Centre for Study of International Affairs (Europe and America) was established by Middlesex University in 1995 to promote study of the transatlantic relationship and to develop postgraduate work in international relations. Members of the Centre's Advisory Board include: Sir Oliver Wright GCMG GCVO DSC (Chairman); Rt Hon. the Lord Ryder of Wenum OBE; The Hon. Edward Streator; Richard Balfe MEP; Nicholas

Harvey MP; Alan Lee Williams OBE; Dr William Schneider Jr; Professor Gary L. McDowell; Professor Joseph A McKinney; Professor Geoffrey Lee Williams; William Mader; Peter Robinson; Geoffrey Smith; Dr Melvyn Stokes. Head of the Centre: Douglas Eden.

Notes on the Contributors

Martin J. Dedman is Senior Lecturer in Economic History at the Middlesex University Business School. He is author of *The Origins and Development of the European Union 1945–95: a History of European Integration* (1996) and other books. He contributed to the Centre's first volume, *The Future of the Atlantic Community* (1997).

Douglas Eden is Head of the Centre for Study of International Affairs (Europe & America) and Principal Lecturer in International History and Politics at Middlesex University, London, and organiser of the annual Trent Park conferences on The Future of the Atlantic Community. A Senior Fellow of the Atlantic Council of the United Kingdom, he is a writer, lecturer and consultant on the politics and cultural aspects of the transatlantic relationship. Among his previous publications, he edited and co-authored the Centre's first volume, *The Future of the Atlantic Community* (1997), *Political Change in Europe* (1981) and contributed on 'Democracy' to *The Reader's Guide to American History*, Peter J. Parish, ed. (1997). He served as a Member of the Greater London Council, 1973–77, and as Chairman of the Heathrow Airport Consultative Committee, 1973–97.

Martin Holmes is Senior Lecturer in Political Economy and Director of the College of Business Administration (UNL) Programme, Mansfield College, Oxford. He has written five books on British political economy and served as a consultant to the US Agency for International Development. He is a co-chairman of the Bruges Group and frequent contributor to its publications. He contributed a chapter to the Centre's first volume, *The Future of the Atlantic Community* (1997).

Joseph A. McKinney is Ben H. Williams Professor of International Economics at Baylor University and was 1996 Fulbright Senior Scholar at Middlesex University. An authority on NAFTA, he testified before Congressional and state legislative committees and the US International Trade Commission and co-directed a research project for the Joint Economic Committee of the US Congress. He has many publications on international trade policy and contributed a chapter to the Centre's previous volume, *The Future of the Atlantic Community* (1997). He is a Member of the Centre's Advisory Board.

William Mader is a consultant in international affairs, specialising on Central and Eastern Europe, Central Asia and the Middle East. He was *Time* magazine's London bureau chief and European diplomatic editor, 1989–93, previously having been chief diplomatic correspondent. He also served as Bonn bureau chief, chief Canadian correspondent, Senior State Department correspondent and Eastern Europe bureau chief. He is a Member of the Advisory Board of the Centre for Study of International Affairs (Europe and America), Middlesex University.

Don E. Newquist, a Democrat from Texas, was nominated to the United States International Trade Commission by President Reagan and confirmed by the Senate in 1988. He was appointed Chairman of the Commission by President Bush for a term from 1991 to 1994. He retired as a Commissioner in December 1997. He is President (United States) of the North American Institute, a private non-profit multi-national organisation exploring the emerging North American regional relationship between the US, Canada and Mexico.

P.J. Priestley has been Head of the North America Department at the Foreign and Commonwealth Office responsible for relations with the United States and Canada since 1996. Formerly, he was HM Consul-General in Geneva, Ambassador in Libreville and held other FCO posts in London and in the Philippines, New Zealand, Zaire and Bulgaria. He holds the title CBE.

William Schneider, Jr is President of International Planning Services Inc., Arlington, Virginia, USA. A member of the Rumsfeld Commission to Assess the Ballistic Missile Threat since 1996, he was US Under-Secretary of State for Security Assistance, Science and Technology, 1983–87, Chairman of the President's General Advisory Committee on Arms Control and Disarmament, 1987–93, and Chairman of the State Department's Defense Trade Advisory Group since 1993. Deputy Director (to Herman Kahn) of the Hudson Institute prior to 1981, he left on appointment by President Reagan to the Office of Management and Budget. He is a Member of the Advisory Board of the Centre for Study of International Affairs (Europe and America), Middlesex University.

Alan Lee Williams is Director of The Atlantic Council of the United Kingdom and Chairman of the European Working Group of the Centre for Strategic and International Studies, Washington, DC. Formerly, he was Warden and Chief Executive of Toynbee Hall and, before that, Director-General of the English-Speaking Union of the Commonwealth. Previously Member of Parliament (Labour) for Hornchurch, he served as Parliamentary Private Secretary to the Secretary of State for Defence (Denis Healey) and, subsequently, to the Secretary of State for Northern Ireland. He was Chairman of the Parliamentary Labour Party Defence Group, 1975–79. He is a Fellow of the Royal Society of Arts and a Member of the Advisory Board of the Centre for Study of International Affairs (Europe and America), Middlesex University. He contributed to the Centre's previous volume, *The Future of the Atlantic Community* (1997). He holds the title OBE.

Geoffrey Lee Williams is Director of the Cambridge-based Institute of Economic and Political Studies. He is also an associate lecturer in international relations at the Centre of International Studies, Cambridge University. Professor Williams was formerly Head of International Relations at Surrey University. He is a former defence consultant to the MoD and NATO Defence Fellow. He has published a growing number of major books on defence and strategic issues and is currently completing *NATO and the Transatlantic Alliance in the Twenty-First Century*, to be published by Macmillan in 2000. He is a Member of the Advisory Board of the Centre for the Study of International Affairs (Europe and America), Middlesex University.

1
NATO and the Atlantic Relationship

Douglas Eden

The Atlantic relationship has come under increasing stress since the collapse of the Soviet Union and the end of the Cold War. The removal of the bipolar world has liberated Europe's nation-states to pursue narrow national interests without fear of offending allies and endangering national security. Commercial and security disagreements between NATO allies which were blurred, fudged or masked in the cause of common security are now pursued with a will. Suppressed resentments are now vented, rivalries renewed and national identities reviewed.

Cold War professions of shared democratic ideals have given way to reveal a variety of national values and cultural differences in the definition, practice and perception of democracy, liberty, freedom, citizenship, individualism and the role of the state. These cultural differences are not only evident in the relationship between Europeans and North Americans, but can be found in the interstate politics of the European Union and the strains on the coherence of, for example, the British, Spanish and Canadian nation-states.

The Soviet Union and its Warsaw Pact having dissolved, the multinational institution most obviously affected by the end of the Cold War is the North Atlantic Treaty Organisation. NATO, which celebrated its fiftieth anniversary in April 1999, was conceived as a purely defensive alliance of independent sovereign states and served its members in this role throughout the Cold War. At the time of the Soviet Union's collapse, NATO had never fired a shot in anger, had never devised plans for initiating a war or unprovoked attack and had never strayed from its posture as a defence organisation. The end of the Soviet threat therefore seemed to beg the question of NATO's validity, utility and survival. That question is still under discussion. Any attempt to answer it must recognise the substance of NATO's traditional role and examine the present and future relationships of its members to each other and the wider world.

NATO was always much more than a defence organisation. Since 1949, it has been the principal multinational institution representing America's commitment to Europe's postwar regeneration, prosperity and security; objectives deemed essential to America's national security and economic well-being. It took two world wars and the advent of the Cold War for the American people to come to accept that the most dangerous international threat to their own national security and prosperity lay in the domination of Europe by a single antagonistic power. By 1945, only the United States herself could ensure this did not happen. With Europe bankrupt and prostrate in every respect and vulnerable to domination by a totalitarian power that would isolate and threaten American democracy, the United States had no choice but to become permanently and effectively a European power. With the end of the Cold War, it is possible for Americans to ask whether such a threat is any longer conceivable; but the Atlantic relationship has become increasingly complex and symbiotic, involving extensive commercial and security interests. In so far as this Atlantic Community has a collective identity, it is expressed largely through the institutions of NATO.

For Europeans, the alliance was the best hope of ensuring a permanent American commitment to the creation of a new, secure and prosperous Europe, and NATO came to be the one institution dedicated exclusively to sustaining the transatlantic link and constructing an Atlantic Community. As NATO's first Secretary-General, General Lord Ismay, once observed from the British point of view, the purpose of NATO was 'to keep the Americans in, the Russians out and the Germans down'. It has long been in Europe's interest for the United States, the major force for stability in the world, to be a European power. Had the United States seen itself as such in 1914 and the 1930s, neither Germany nor any other European state could have contemplated aggrandising itself by war.

At the time of NATO's foundation, the United States viewed its commitment as politically supportive and did not contemplate stationing significant forces in Europe. Indeed, the initial understanding was that the United States contribution would be in the form of political weight to reinforce its economic support for Europe's reconstruction and security. The Europeans were to provide the manpower and the bulk of the *matériel* for their own defence. This understanding was never honoured by the Europeans, and the result was America's eventually extensive commitment of men, *matériel* and technology to the defence of Europe. The argument across the Atlantic over defence burden-sharing has been a constant feature of the relationship for 50 years. America's commercial and political commitments to Europe preceded her more reluctant military commitment, reflecting her residual desire for a time when Europe might cease to be a burden to the American taxpayer and assume a role as a cooperative economic partner responsible for its own defence. Perhaps, it was thought, the United States might again one day shelter behind her Atlantic wall, knowing a friendly democratic free-enterprise Europe secured the eastern shore. Some Americans still harbour such hopes.

The American desire that Europe should be less dependent on the American taxpayer and that extreme nationalism or Franco-German rivalry should not again draw her into a European war led the United States to favour greater cooperation and even union among the Western European nation-states. European integration, from the days of the European Communities to today's European Union, has consequently been encouraged and underwritten by American policy. This was a major economic and political strategy, with security implications. It was launched by the Marshall Plan in 1947, which required the Europeans to formulate cooperative proposals for American investment in their reconstruction, and has continued for more than 50 years. The United States would undoubtedly have evolved this policy even without the threat posed to the weakened Western European states by Soviet subversion. However, Soviet antagonism was the direct and immediate cause of NATO's foundation.

The Soviet danger has disappeared, but mutual mistrust and potential insecurity among Europe's states continues to be allayed by the American commitment through NATO. NATO provided guarantees from the outset not only against Soviet expansion in Europe, but also against internecine conflict on the Western side of the iron curtain. Once Soviet hegemony disintegrated, former satellites and some of the former Soviet republics sought from the United States similar protection to that enjoyed by NATO members. All wished to share the sense of Europe as a war-free zone, but in all cases it was the involvement of the United States that made NATO especially attractive.

America, the only European power without European territory, is the one referee acceptable to European states concerned about instability and the security of their independence and borders. The American role in Northern Ireland is one clear example. There are others. Poland and the Czech Republic, in applying to join NATO, were principally concerned to insure themselves against the resurgence of a newly expansionist Russia; but they are also concerned to avoid exchanging Soviet domination for German. Germany's power is safely allocated to NATO under American leadership, and a strong American commercial and political presence obviates the restoration of a monopolistic German sphere of influence in Eastern Europe.

Germany is indeed anxious to establish a role in Europe that does not antagonise or alarm any of her neighbours. This has been achieved with respect to her neighbours to the north, west and south by her zealous membership of the European Union and the North Atlantic Treaty Organisation.[1] Relations to the east are a bit more problematic. Reunited Germany is only about two-thirds the size of the Weimar Republic. The remainder lies to Germany's east. Nearly one-third of German territory prior to Hitler's expansion is now Polish territory and millions of Germans are refugees or descendants of refugees from those lands or the Sudetenland of Bohemia. In these circumstances, the new Germany is keen to assure her eastern neighbours that renewing cultural and commercial ties does not involve the revival of German hegemony or irredentism. That insurance policy is provided by NATO and Germany's alliance with the United States. The accession to NATO of Poland, the Czech Republic and Hungary in 1999 provided reinsurance.

During the events that led to the reunification of West and East Germany and during the formation of the Franco-German relationship that dominates the European Union, it was the United States that held the ring and guaranteed the stable environment that made these outcomes possible. NATO was the essential institution by which American power and influence could be deployed effectively and acceptably in Europe. On the other hand, the alliance most of the time provided the world's only democratic superpower with a base of friendly political support that helped her avoid isolation and uncertainty in her global role.

America's leadership of NATO may flow from her political, economic, cultural and military power, but her military status does not derive solely from her wealth, manpower and weaponry. Her technological leadership and will to invest in it and sustain it is vital to NATO. She has developed immensely sophisticated armaments which have startled the world since they were first publicly and dramatically displayed during the Gulf War of 1991, and she has produced communications, command and control systems that no other country or group of nations is either willing or can afford to replicate. In projecting power today, whether in warfare or peacekeeping, these extremely expensive systems are unsurpassable.

America's allies have access to these systems only through bilateral understandings or through NATO joint operations. Elements under US control were essential to the British effort in the 1982 Falklands War and to the coalition that liberated Kuwait in 1991. They still serve the forces containing Saddam Hussein. However, the importance of the systems assigned to NATO only became evident after the Atlantic alliance deployed forces to Bosnia in 1995 and launched the first combat operations in NATO history, against the Federal Republic of Yugoslavia, in 1999. NATO would be unimaginable without the United States in any case, but it is also true that the other member states could not mobilise, deploy and manage any complex military undertaking without the American command and control systems.

This dependence on American technology has been further reinforced by the discovery of the extensive proliferation of weapons of mass destruction (WMDs) and the ballistic missiles that can deliver them to targets in most parts of the world. During 1998, successful nuclear tests by Pakistan and India signified the spreading of nuclear weapon technology, and the successful launch of a multi-stage ballistic missile over Japan by North Korea provided alarming and public evidence of proliferation. An authoritative official report[2] for the US government in July 1998 on the ballistic missile and WMD threats, quickly passed to European allies, led to defence strategy reviews being reopened in Western capitals and to a new reliance on the United States to produce defensive answers to an increasing menace that particularly threatens Europe. Britain and Germany informed Washington that they wished to contribute to any counter-measures. The President soon requested and Congress quickly appropriated an initial amount to explore development of a strategic defence system to thwart missile attacks by rogue states.

On the whole, dependence on US technology has not been a problem for at least two of Europe's great NATO powers, Britain and Germany; but it is a different matter for France. The Gaullist tradition has always been concerned with what it sometimes calls 'American hegemony' and has insisted that France must retain complete independence of action. Although France has not participated in NATO's military command structure since President De Gaulle withdrew in 1966, she has always retained the protection of the alliance and maintained a discreet, even secret, involvement in allied military planning.[3]

While NATO did not engage in warfare, France could indulge her 'independence' and sense of solitary grandeur without facing up to the reality of her position. This luxury ended with NATO's first punitive military action: Operation Allied Force against Yugoslavia in 1999. Any alliance members dubious about their willingness to accept American leadership in European security matters were put on the spot. One reporter commented, 'The stark realisation that Europe is powerless without American support has come as a shock to a country brought up on the nationalist legacy of General De Gaulle.'[4] As many as 90 French aircraft were flying missions over Serbia, guided by the American command and control systems allocated to NATO, much to the shock of many French citizens who had assumed that France had the capacity to act independently of the United States. Gaullists decried 'the obliteration of France' and accused President Chirac of 'copying the "complacent" and "self-effacing" British'.[5]

For years, France had tried to convince her European allies to establish a European defence force separate from NATO and American leadership, but Germany and Britain, her most important allies, and others, repeatedly refused to undermine NATO and the strong link to the United States. Consequently, the Gaullist Chirac began to move closer to NATO, even contemplating rejoining the military command structure. The course of events in the former Yugoslavia before American involvement demonstrated the inability of the European powers to police their region without the United States. By committing units to Operation Allied Force, France explicitly recognised this for the first time. For Germany, participating in the campaign against Yugoslavia was her first time in combat since 1945, a poignant testimony of her attachment to NATO and her restoration as a great power.

Occasional ambivalence by NATO's European members toward their relationship with the United States is matched by American ambivalence. On the one hand, the United States wants its European allies to spend more on defence, bear a greater share of the collective defence burden (usually referred to by American legislators as a 'fair' share) and take greater responsibility for maintaining stability in Europe. On the other hand, the US reacts against the vision of a strong 'European pillar' that acts independently and separately from NATO and the American partnership.

Generally, the British and Germans side with the United States; but pressures for European Union integration, including a common foreign and defence policy, have led both, with Washington's encouragement, to seek a 'European Security and Defence Identity' (ESDI) with France, providing the foundation for a Common Defence and Security Policy (CDSP) for the European Union.[6] This would allow the European allies to lead NATO peacekeeping and crisis management operations in their region, using America's NATO command, control and communications systems, without necessarily involving North American troops. The supposition is that the United States would be reassured that her interests would be protected because of the continued dependence on US control systems and the routing of proposed operations through NATO policy and planning procedures.[7] She would be gratified by Europe's evident willingness to carry a larger burden. It is perhaps significant that Britain, so long seen by France as little better than an American security puppet, joined France in launching an ESDI initiative at their St Mâlo summit in December 1998.

One early earnest of this new policy was the contribution by the Europeans of 85 per cent of the troops in the provisional Kosovo peace-keeping force that NATO sent to stand by in Macedonia in 1998–99. Belgrade's pre-emptive ethnic cleansing campaign in Kosovo and the NATO response that ensued in March 1999 rather altered the mission and size of that force. The effect of this experience on NATO's ESDI plans has, at the time of writing, yet to be fully assessed; however, it is already apparent that support for the scheme has grown among the principal players on both sides of the Atlantic. This is evidenced by the Europeans accepting a leading responsibility in the postwar K-For peacekeeping mission and the 'Marshall Plan' for the Balkans.

For some European members of NATO, the alliance provides a useful diplomatic tool to achieve objectives they do not wish to pursue through the European Union. This can be somewhat irritating for the United States. France, for example, has long opposed the enlargement of the EU and has supported NATO enlargement as an alternative.[8] Germany, for example, would prefer to gain access to Romanian gas by admitting Romania to NATO rather than admit her to the EU. NATO membership provides stability and thus makes investment in member states safe. EU membership entitles citizens of member states to free movement any-where in the Union. It is attractive to Germany to develop Romanian gas-fields without having to accommodate Romanian immigrants. Also, the financial cost of NATO enlargement is less for European NATO members and non-members than the cost of EU enlargement, while the US and Canada share the cost of NATO enlargement as well as bearing an increase in their security commitments. It remains to be seen whether the EU posture toward Romania and Bulgaria, and other Balkan states, may not have been altered by the Kosovo campaign, in which they played roles supportive of NATO.

For the United States, another question is whether she can convince her NATO partners to share her global concerns and responsibilities. Many of these are at least as important to the vital interests of the Europeans: for example, free access to Middle East oil (also crucial to Japan) and preventing unfriendly states from blackmailing allies or threatening their interests with terrorism, weapons of mass destruction or aggression outside Europe.

Prior to Operation Allied Force, Washington hoped that NATO's involvement in the Balkans would provide a precedent for a 'new strategic concept' of the alliance. This would involve extending NATO's mission beyond its traditional defence of allied territory. The new NATO would be as much 'an alliance of interests' to protect agreed North American and European interests from a variety of existing and potential problems and threats inside and outside Europe. These would include, for example, the proliferation of nuclear, chemical and biological weapons and their delivery systems, troublemaking by 'rogue states', international terrorism and drug trafficking. This agenda was foreshadowed in former Secretary of State Warren Christopher's speech to the June 1995 NATO conference in Madrid, when he called for 'the integration of the economies of North America and Europe' and 'common economic and political action to expand democracy, prosperity and stability.'

Prior to the semi-centennial NATO summit in April 1999, one NATO senior official was quoted as saying, 'when America talks of the defence of interests, and not just territories, it leads to continued suspicions that the United States is seeking to globalise NATO. NATO is still Euro-Atlantic, but we should not artificially exclude what we might use NATO for'.[9] Some European officials were reported to be suspicious that the United States might exaggerate threats such as proliferation of weapons of mass destruction to frighten European populations into allowing NATO to become a global organisation. US Secretary of State Madeleine Albright has tried to assure the allies that future NATO missions would take them a bit further afield, but not all over the world; but the reluctance of NATO's European members to invest in new equipment or even to sustain levels of military expenditure casts massive doubts over the reality of any ESDI proposal, let alone the ability of Europe to play an effective role in any serious projection of NATO power outside the traditional alliance defence perimeter.[10] Nevertheless, the NATO allies unanimously adopted the new NATO doctrine of peace enforcement, the 'Strategic Concept', at the April 1999 Washington Conference that celebrated the alliance's fiftieth anniversary. At that moment, in the midst of the conflict with Yugoslavia, NATO officially ceased to be a purely defensive alliance. The success of Operation Allied Force against Yugoslavia in 1999 answered many questions about the future capacity, cohesion, resolve and survivability of NATO.

A longstanding feature of the transatlantic relationship has been the unwritten understanding that America's security guarantees to Europe entitle her to access to European markets. The suspicion is growing, and not only in the United States, that the European Union may be developing into a more protectionist and exclusive bloc than in the past. Efforts to develop a Transatlantic Free Trade Area have been stalled in Europe despite the huge importance of Atlantic trading and investment relationships,[11] and serious trade disputes have begun to threaten good commercial relations. Dissatisfaction has grown in the United States with the reluctance of some European countries to expand their economies, to reduce impediments to freer trade and to share responsibility for reviving the world economy after the economic crises in Japan, the Pacific Rim countries and South America. The desire in some European circles to move along the spectrum of the transatlantic relationship from partnership toward rivalry and even antagonism is causing concern.[12] This is reflected in French resistance to the negotiation of a New Transatlantic Marketplace (NTM)[13] and in pressure to create an exclusively European power-centre that might threaten the cohesion of NATO.

Periodic emergencies such as Bosnia and Kosovo, and the recent revelations of WMD and ballistic missile proliferation, brusquely remind Europeans of their need for American partnership; but such alarms do not appear to quench the desire by some Europeans to build a rival to American power and oppose a perceived American cultural threat. The clear and present danger of the Soviet threat during the Cold War led the European elites to restrain their nationalisms, ambitions and transatlantic antagonisms in order to preserve the American security guarantee against mortal peril. Without the danger, it is more difficult to maintain the discipline.

Most Europeans who wish European union to stop short of political integration appreciate the transatlantic links. Those who pursue the ideal of a politically united Europe should understand that they can only hope to achieve their goal in partnership with the United States. They must accept the reality of Europe's need for the American alliance and not separate Europe from America. Americans are largely neutral on questions of European Union integration, except for impatience with attempts to construct a Union that is exclusive and vaingloriously aims to rival and limit rather than partner and share American power and influence.

There is no chance that a European Union superpower will appear. America will find a superpower rival soon enough – perhaps in less than 20 years – in a China with a population larger than North America's and Western Europe's put together, but unlikely to be a Western-style democracy. Europe and North America will need each other as much as they ever did. The hope must be that both appreciate this and that neither America's traditional isolationism nor the historic faults in Europe's political culture will undermine the North Atlantic project.

NATO, as in the past, will only survive and grow as the alliance of democracies. The fissures in the alliance opened by illiberal protectionism, nationalism and political and cultural rivalry should be healed and the humanitarian ideals that guided the alliance through the Cold War should be refreshed. If Europe is to achieve more equal partnership with the United States in a North Atlantic Treaty Organisation that remains relevant and successful, Europeans need to forswear both narrow nationalism and Euro-nationalism and be guided by transatlantic democratic values. They will also have to show greater willingness to meet the cost of complete integration into NATO's command and control system and to work with the United States inside and outside Europe wherever alliance members' interests coincide.[14]

As NATO passed its fiftieth anniversary, the Atlantic Community was passing through a watershed. It is difficult to see how the Europeans alone can create anything of equivalent value to put in place of the American alliance. NATO has come a long way since Lord Ismay's trenchant description of its mission. The North American involvement in European affairs has been crucial to Europe's recovery from the aggressive nationalism and repressive collectivism that damaged her so severely in the twentieth century. Members' responses to the new prosperity and the international responsibilities that economic power brings will reveal the future of NATO and the Atlantic relationship, and the prospects for democracy, liberty and stability in Europe and the wider world.

Notes

1   As long ago as 1953, German Chancellor Konrad Adenauer rejected British suggestions for a reunited but neutral Germany because he was convinced that West Germany must be tied to the democratic sheet anchor of American protection rather than risk yet again the demise of democracy in a united Germany. His objective was membership of NATO, which West Germany achieved in 1955, and acceptance of Germany as a full democratic partner by her western neighbours. In place of her discredited nationalism, West Germany's founding *raison d'être* became her alliance with America. She assumed a new identity as the 'best' European and her national interests were pursued in the name of 'Europe' and the North Atlantic. See Anthony Glees, 'Churchill's Last Gambit' (based on secret documents released under the Thirty Year Rule at

the Public Record Office, London) in *Encounter* 44:4, April 1985, pp. 27–35. Also, Thomas A Schwartz, 'The United States and Germany after 1945', in *Diplomatic History* 19:4, Fall 1995, pp. 549–68. Since reunification in 1991, however, Germany has reordered the priority of her most important relationships, giving a higher priority to her relationship with France than to the one with America.

2 *Report of the Commission to Assess the Ballistic Missile Threat to the United States: Executive Summary* (Washington, DC: US Government Printing Office, 15 July 1998, web address: http://www.access.gpo.gov/su_docs/newnote.html). The Commission was established under the National Defense Authorization Act for Fiscal Year 1997 and its members were nominated by the leaderships of both Houses of Congress and appointed by the Director of Central Intelligence on behalf of the President. Also, see William Schneider, Jr (a member of the Commission), 'Europe Comes into Range' in *The Financial Times*, 25 August 1998, p. 10.

3 For a summary of France's partial withdrawal from NATO, see Ronald E Powaski, *The Entangling Alliance: the United States and European Security, 1950–1993* (Westport, Connecticut, and London: Greenwood Press, 1994), pp. 75–8.

4 Adam Sage, 'France struggles with loss of its "grand solitude"', *The Times*, 31 March 1999, p. 5.

5 Ibid. The French contribution to the air war in terms of aircraft allocated was second only to the massive American presence. It makes a striking comparison with the British contribution of approximately 35 aircraft until it is noted that the British flew many more missions than the French. Britain had invested in compatible advanced technology and so could integrate into the US-supplied CCC system and thus be far more effective with fewer aircraft than France. The French, who had not made the necessary investments over the years, were unable to participate easily or fully in NATO's air assault despite the large number of aircraft they allocated to the operation.

6 It is significant that the NATO Secretary-General, Javier Solana, was selected in May 1999 to be the first head of the CSDP; thus ensuring a smooth evolution of the EU's CSDP with ESDI in harmony with NATO.

7 See Javier Solana, NATO Secretary-General: 'The Washington Summit: NATO steps boldly into the 21st century' in *NATO Review* 47:1, Spring 1999, p. 6. Also, 'Growing the Alliance' in *The Economist*, 13 March 1999, p. 24.

8 French motivations include the desire to contain German power and maintain French influence on German policy. EU expansion would initially be in Germany's traditional sphere of commercial and political influence and thus be likely to increase Germany's rather than France's power in the European Union.

9 Roger Cohen, 'Europeans Contest US NATO Vision', *International Herald Tribune*, 28 November 1998, p. 1.

10 Ibid. See also, William Pfaff, 'Washington's New Vision for NATO Could be Divisive', *International Herald Tribune*, 5 December 1998, p. 8; and 'Platform envy' and 'NATO's mid-life crisis' in *The Economist*, 12 December 1998.

11 See Dr Robert A. Rogowsky, 'Converging Competition Policies in the Transatlantic Marketplace' in Douglas Eden, ed., *The Future of the Atlantic Community* (London: Middlesex University Press, 1997), pp. 54–74.

12 See 'When the snarling's over', in *The Economist*, 13 March 1999, p. 18.

13 In vetoing the NTM, France also barred progress toward a Transatlantic Free
    Trade Area (TAFTA), which is supported by Britain and Germany. The object-
    ives of a TAFTA or some lesser form of transatlantic trading equivalent of
    NATO are at least as political as commercial, helping to cement the Atlantic
    relationship in the aftermath of the Cold War. Nearly all Atlanticists want to
    see progress in this direction. James Sperling and Emil Kirchner, for example,
    claim that European stability depends on a 'congruence and interdepend-
    ence' of economic and military institutions within the North Atlantic alliance
    to produce 'a common political and economic frame of reference' without
    which Europe will fail to achieve unity or 'a co-operative pan-European
    security order'. See their article, 'Economic security and the problem of co-
    operation in post-Cold War Europe', in *Review of International Studies (1998)*,
    no. 24, pp. 221–37; and their book, *Recasting the European Order: Security
    Architectures and Economic Co-operation* (Manchester: Manchester University
    Press, 1997). There is at least one non-French scholar who puts forward the
    view that, although it was probably not the French intention to assist the
    Atlantic relationship, it was in the Euro-American interest to sink the NTM
    proposal. As a result, he claims, the European Commission produced instead
    the Draft Action Plan for Transatlantic Economic Partnership, in his view a
    better because less institutional framework for transatlantic trade relations
    (Brian Hindley, 'Transatlantic Trade Relations', *International Affairs* 75:1, Janu-
    ary 1999). Meanwhile, arguments over bananas and hormone-treated beef,
    mainly resulting from a protectionist Europe's reluctance to respect the
    agreed rules of free trade, form the tips of large icebergs that chill transatlantic
    relations.

14 For another extensive discussion, see Margarita Mathiopoulos, 'The USA and
    Europe as Global Players in the 21st Century', in *Aussenpolitik*, English Edition,
    vol. 49, 4th Quarter 1998, pp. 36–49.

2
NATO's Enlargement: Limited, Controversial, Inevitable

William Mader

During the last year of the twentieth century, NATO celebrated, with appropriate commemorative occasions, its fiftieth anniversary. But the alliance in 1999 marked also another salient milestone in its successful history: its controversial enlargement eastwards in the wake of the Cold War's demise. Three new members, all formerly component parts of the now-defunct Warsaw Pact, were admitted. They are the previously Communist-ruled countries of Poland, the Czech Republic and Hungary.

At NATO's summit in Madrid in July 1997, the alliance's heads of government officially gave the green light to the enlargement, formally designating the three Central European nations as prospective new members. With that decision, the painstaking, complex negotiations involved in the admission process began, culminating in the requisite ratification by NATO members' legislatures and the deposition of the trio's accession documents. Also in Madrid, as a result of a compromise, the summit noted in its communiqué that it 'expects to extend further invitations in the coming years to nations willing and able to assume the responsibilities of membership'.

This latest enlargement is the fourth in NATO's history, each representing an important chapter. Originally, the North Atlantic Treaty was signed by 12 nations on 4 April 1949, in response to the emerging Soviet threat, ensuring crucial US commitment to aid in the defence of Western Europe. Greece and Turkey joined in 1952, completing the creation of the alliance's strategic southern flank. West Germany became a member in 1955 as a vital part of its post-Second World War rehabilitation – as well as its being the key front-line state of the West in the Cold War. Spain came into the alliance in 1982, with its recently established democratic credentials, bringing NATO's membership to 16.

The latest addition of the three new members bears, however, a fundamentally different, unprecedented hallmark: it was the first time that former members of the defunct Warsaw Pact became fully fledged partners in NATO. In essence, it recognised their transformation from Communist satellites of the former Soviet Union into democratic societies. Their admission into the alliance did not occur with undue speed. The process took fully a decade, after the collapse of the Communist system in 1989 in Central and South Central Europe.

Contrary to their expectations, their path into NATO was not easy. They were confronted not only with the painful and complex task of complete political, economic and social restructuring, but, after the initial blush of euphoria in the wake of the Communist system's unexpected disintegration in Europe, the issue of their accession triggered controversy within the alliance, as well as new tensions with Moscow. In the exultant mood at the end of the Cold War, the simplistic notion that the former satellite countries would rapidly join Western institutions was equally widely held in the West – even by those who should have known better.

Among the Central and South Central European countries which had just shed the oppressive hand of Communism, this view was given its own special twist. In their own euphoric mood sparked by their having come out into the light from under the dark hand of Communism, they expected virtually immediate acceptance into Western institutions. They saw it almost as a formality. They considered it their just reward – indeed, their right – for having endured Moscow's rule for over four decades, imposed by the Soviet army with Western acquiescence.

But apart from what they regarded as the justice of their case, these former Communist satellites saw historical, political, economic and security reasons for speedily joining, and being automatically accepted by, all Western institutions. This was not a newly discovered attitude. It reflected age-old views deeply embedded in these countries' convictions, thus guiding their mentality and actions.

They consider themselves European by history, culture, tradition and outlook. That they could not be part of Europe after the Second World War but were consigned to the Soviet Empire until its self-induced collapse was not their choice, they argue rightly. Indeed, they believe, again rightly, it was imposed upon them by the capitulation of the US and Britain to Soviet demands at the Yalta summit of 1945. They regard themselves as the traditional easternmost bastions of European civilisation, who had borne their fair share of protecting it. They feel themselves fully European in every sense, historically westward-looking, and expect to be treated as such. They resent deeply its being questioned in the slightest by anyone. Thus, they believe that their joining the gamut of European organisations, particularly NATO and the EU, is their natural right, not just their privilege. They look upon their more than four decades' domination by Moscow, which cut them off from the rest of Europe, as a tragic aberration beyond their choice and control, and which now must be set right.

Their claim to European identity is valid to varying degrees. There is no dispute about it as far as the Central European states – Poland, the Czech Republic, Slovakia, Hungary and Slovenia – and the Baltic republics, with their Hanseatic history, are concerned. To a somewhat lesser extent, it is also true of Romania and Bulgaria; the difference in their case is that they also bear more than a whiff of the Balkans. Ukraine is in a grey area culturally and historically that is more eastwardly oriented. Belarus, which remains an unreconstructed Communist-style state, continues to look eastward to its Russian brother. Consequently, it has no desire to join the West in any form, much to the latter's heartfelt relief. Indeed, Belarus's desire nowadays is to be reintegrated into Russia. Slovakia, under its present dictatorial leadership, shows no inclination to implement serious political reforms. Consequently, as long as that state of affairs lasts, it has no realistic prospect of becoming a part of NATO or the EU.

But apart from these considerations and claims, there are also vital geopolitical factors. In their entire history, the Central and South Central European and Baltic states, by virtue of their geography, have found themselves sandwiched between Germany and Russia, later the Soviet Union, and often suffered for it. In the case of Ukraine, during most of its existence it was part of Russia and subsequently of the Soviet Union. The Baltic states were forcibly integrated into the Soviet Union at the end of the Second World War, after long periods of Russian and then German occupation.

In the deeply rooted convictions of the Central Europeans and the Baltic states, the threats of both Germany and Russia remain as unalloyed as ever. To be sure, Germany nowadays, because of its democratic system and total commitment to NATO, is seen as a latent threat at worst. None the less, these countries have been at best uneasy about heavy German investment in their economies in the wake of the Cold War, albeit quietly because of their need for financial and other assistance. It does explain, however, their incessant clamour for other Western investment as well. They are rightly convinced that with predominant economic influence comes also overweening political influence.

Whether stable or in turmoil, Russia is openly feared, and not only because of its nuclear weapons. Russia's ambition to hold sway over her region – rooted not only in the Communist period but going back to the days of the tsars – is historic. The difference during the Soviet period was that under Stalin it actually came to fruition.

Post-Communist Moscow's virulent diplomatic drive against NATO's enlargement is seen in these countries as reconfirmation of this unabated Russian ambition. Although he was referring directly to his own country, Jan Olszewski, leader of the Movement for the Reconstruction of Poland, and a former post-Communist prime minister, spoke on all these countries' behalf when he said: 'Our membership of a US-led NATO means that we get guarantees that Germany, as part of the alliance, will remain a friendly state, while Russia, thanks to the alliance, can be kept at arm's length.'[1] A high-ranking Hungarian diplomat echoed, 'we want to be in NATO because it means American-led protection against Germany and Russia. They may not be a real threat now, but history has taught us that the future might well be different.' It is this fundamental conviction, in addition to profound economic interests, which is the very substance also of the formerly Communist states' unswerving drive to become members of the European Union. 'The more tightly Germany is tied into NATO and the EU, the more secure we feel. The more deeply we are tied into NATO and the EU, the more secure we are *vis-à-vis* Russia', said a senior Czech diplomat.

Their pursuit of these ambitions has beyond question spurred the Central Europeans and the Baltic republics to implement political and economic reforms with considerable success. It has also prompted them to settle, or at least reduce, centuries of friction with their immediate neighbours. Hungary, for example, has reached agreements with both Slovakia and Romania on the treatment of Hungarian minorities by them. To be sure, these accords have been observed more in the breach, mainly by Slovakia. Still, at least there has been progress on this front. And Budapest has tacitly renounced irredentist demands of former Hungarian territories forming parts of Romania and Slovakia. Poland has resolved its border disputes with Ukraine, leading to pronouncedly friendly relations between them. The Baltic states, albeit under quiet but determined doses of Western pressure, have at least somewhat eased the lot of their large Russian minorities, and Lithuania and Poland have also solved their mutual territorial disputes.

The NATO summit's decision in July 1997 to admit Poland, the Czech Republic and Hungary as new members from among the applicants was no surprise; its evolution was lengthy and widely trailed. The reasons for this decision were basically sound. These three countries were the best qualified among those pushing for NATO membership. They established democratic credentials; moved a considerable distance, although with some setbacks, along the path of economic and social reforms; and reconstructed their military establishments, albeit with varying degrees of success. Of the three, Poland and Hungary showed the most progress on all counts, the Czech Republic the least on the military and economic fronts. Poland's inclusion was also essential simply because of its key geopolitical position as the largest Central European country, situated between Germany and Russia. 'If Poland had not been ready, the others would have had to wait until it was', said a high-ranking British diplomat. And in any case, the US, because of its large domestic constituency of Polish origin, and Germany, because of its unremitting drive for full reconciliation with the Poles, were determined to ensure that Poland was the first, or among the first, to be admitted.

The Baltic states, as so often in their history, found themselves benighted by their geographical location. Precisely because they are three small states on the periphery of Russia, from the moment of their post-Communist independence they have been clamouring for NATO membership. 'Our priority is simple: NATO', said a senior Latvian diplomat. 'It's dictated by realities.' But just as precisely these realities, as the West sees them, keep them outside the alliance. They meet the political, economic and, as far as their tiny armed forces go, military criteria. Their misfortune is to be regarded by the West, although no Western official will publicly say so, as being too small to be of decisive strategic significance yet also too sensitive an issue *vis-à-vis* Russia.

Indeed, even in the last breath of Mikhail Gorbachev's reign, as Communism was serially toppled first across Central and South Central Europe, the Soviet Union vehemently opposed any NATO enlargement eastwards. It is a policy that also remained resolutely firm under Boris Yeltsin, and no doubt will continue to be so under his successor. The former Russian Prime and Foreign Minister, Yevgeny Primakov, as his predecessors, never tired of maintaining that Moscow got a firm pledge from US President George Bush that NATO would not push its boundary toward the east, only to see it violated. For its part, the US has firmly denied having made this commitment. Primakov has admitted that no such promise was given in writing, but has claimed a verbal pledge was made. So much for the word of a gentleman, he has implied in wounded tones.

In any case, what is clear is that the US and its allies from the onset of Communism's collapse in Central and South Central Europe publicly declared NATO's and the EU's doors to be open to those regions' countries. Once sobered up from their euphoria, inevitable arguments began among NATO governments as to whether enlargement should occur, and, if so, how far it should extend geographically. NATO's European members themselves were disunited on the matter and, indeed, to a lesser extent remain so. The Clinton Administration, at its outset and characteristically since, has compounded the problem by offering no clear leadership. It has swung from one extreme to the other. First it argued for the admission of virtually anyone formerly in the Soviet Empire, even the newly-independent Central Asian states. Then, in a typical U-turn, it questioned any enlargement, with the possible exception of Poland, as Russia's opposition remained loud and resolute. And then once again it switched back to arguing that eventual Russian membership should not be foreclosed, a position it has not yet abandoned. None the less, and mainly as a result of assiduous British and German diplomacy, a unanimous NATO decision was reached for a limited 'first wave' expansion.

Being hard and Byzantine bargainers, the Russians played their cards superbly well, especially given their extremely weak position. As a number of Russian officials and politicians privately acknowledged, Russia was not in a position to block enlargement if NATO was determined to go ahead with it. But what Russia could do was to limit its geographical scope, and gain an effective and important say in the alliance's affairs. 'If we had won the Cold War, we wouldn't have been concerned about the losers', admitted a Russian diplomat. 'We would have taken all we could swallow.' Doubtless an accurate assessment.

As it is, the Russians succeeded in convincing NATO that admitting the Baltic states, or any other part of the former Soviet Union, would be a step too far. Even if Russia, for the time being, is not militarily in a position to resist such a broad enlargement of the alliance, it would result in severe tensions with the West, verging on a renewed Cold War, Moscow argued vehemently. Western capitals, anxious to avoid serious strains with Moscow, lest it jeopardise Russia's internal reforms (such as they were), bowed to the argument. More than that, Russia adroitly extracted huge concessions from the West, which affect NATO's role and ability to perform its functions.

The Founding Act on Mutual Relations, Co-operation and Security between NATO and Russia, signed in Paris on 27 May 1997, enshrines Moscow's gains. It sets up a permanent joint council of the allies and Russia; it provides for consultation and coordination, and it calls also for joint decision-making and action on security issues of common concern.

The Clinton Administration's plainly defensive mantra is that this amounts to a Russian voice, but not a veto. However, in reality it is an implicit Russian veto. For it is difficult to imagine that Russia will not exercise, and even bend where it can, its right to disagree, and thereby do its best to block or at least inhibit any NATO action that displeases it.

Given the nature of the newly formed joint council, Henry Kissinger was right in insisting that 'Russian acquiescence to a decision (enlargement) that Moscow is in no position to prevent was achieved at an exorbitant price.'[2] Yeltsin was right, too, when he said that the Founding Act meant that 'the way we (in the council) solve . . . issues is by consensus. That's how it is today among the NATO countries.'[3] Thus, a senior British diplomat accurately described the Founding Act as 'closely resembling Russian membership in NATO'. For the Central and South Central Europeans and the Baltic states, this new arrangement between NATO and Russia is deeply worrying – a concern understandably shared by Ukraine. From their point of view, it starkly guarantees a Russian say in NATO's affairs, directly affecting them, not least the three new Central European members. Given current political trends in Russia, with the re-emergence of an increasingly chauvinistic and anti-Western mood, both traditional features in its history, the implications for the West are obviously not what it wanted to attain through its concessions to Moscow.

In view of this situation, the question is, will NATO be able to perform as originally intended? That is, will it be able to act rapidly and effectively against a threat or attack? Under Article 5 of the North Atlantic Treaty, an external attack on one member is an attack on all. The assumption – a vital assumption – is that Article 5 remains intact in every sense, and any Russian attempt to dilute it will be ignored. That is easier to say than to do. In light of the NATO–Russia accord, it depends on individual NATO members' perceptions of Russian moves whether they can quickly, or at all, reach unanimous decisions against them. While NATO reshapes itself militarily and variegates its role into, among others, peacekeeping out of its area (as in Bosnia, for instance) and combating terrorism and drug trafficking, it is essential that its original charter be fulfilled. It must continue, above all, as a defensive organisation, rapidly able to prevent or defeat any design against its cohesion or attack against its members.

Not surprisingly, it is a fundamentally unaltered NATO that the Central Europeans and other former Communist-ruled European countries want to join. 'We cannot protect ourselves by ourselves against encroaching influence from the East, let alone a large-scale attack', said a Czech diplomat. 'We are willing to do our share, but we need to be inside NATO for genuine protection.' And in their minds, the Central and South Central Europeans and the Baltic republics see Russia, even if in the longer term, as the most likely source of any renewed threat in whatever form. 'The Russian military is a shambles now, but it will not be such for ever', warned the same diplomat. It also remains a nuclear power and, amid its internal turmoil, an increasingly unsafe one. And it is reasonable to assume that Russia's desire to hold sway over Central and South Central Europe, as well as the Baltic states and the Ukraine, will not diminish, whatever its internal situation and changes at the top.

Western opponents of NATO's enlargement form two camps. One insists that the benefits are outweighed by the severity of tensions it introduces and exacerbates in relations with Russia. This view maintains that it is an unnecessary provocation of an understandably worried Russia beset by weakness. The other group argues that even limiting admission to the three Central European states makes the alliance too unwieldy, too diluted. Both schools of thought include distinguished politicians, diplomats, military men and academics with considerable knowledge and experience in Russian affairs. However, in the end both groups were defeated by NATO's decision to enlarge its membership.

The NATO summit's decision on enlargement was a bitter pill for the excluded to swallow. Led by the US, the summit tried to soothe the Baltic states, Romania, Bulgaria and Slovenia by stressing that the door remained open for future admissions. Ukraine, which has been equally eager to join but has wisely understood that its geopolitical position at least for the time being rules that out, was offered another consolation prize as well. This was granted in recognition of Ukraine's size and strategic position. Thus, at the time of the summit, a Charter of Distinctive Partnership was signed between NATO and Ukraine. It set up the NATO–Ukraine Commission, which is to meet at least twice annually; it allows for close cooperation in peacekeeping; it calls for consultation on political and security-related issues; and it guarantees collaboration against drug trafficking and terrorism. 'We understand that being situated next to Russia makes it impossible for us to join at this stage', said a high-ranking Ukrainian diplomat. 'We can't afford to irritate the Russians too much. We have a large Russian minority within our borders and other, very sensitive, unresolved issues with Moscow. But we can always hope.'

The Baltic states, somewhat belatedly, have also realised that their understandably strident demand to be included in NATO's enlargement has not only been unavailing, but to some extent even counter-productive. 'There are times when it makes sense to make a nuisance of yourself.

And there are times when it does not', said a high-ranking British diplomat. 'The Baltics are just starting to comprehend that they have over-done it a bit.' There are occasions when, for the sake of not embarrassing one's big-power supporters, it is better not to push too hard. This much is now acknowledged privately by some officials and politicians from the Baltic republics. At the same time, the Baltics' clamour to be admitted into the alliance is fully understandable, given their past experiences. US Secretary of State Madeleine Albright's repeated assurances that they are 'serious candidates' for NATO membership amount to nothing more than a palliative and the Baltic republics suspect as much.

There is no wish within NATO to admit the Baltic republics in the foreseeable future. 'If they were not in such an isolated location and right next door to Russia, things could be different', explained an American diplomat. This, of course, does not exclude the Baltic states from joining the EU and other European institutions. Indeed, Estonia already has a place on the next wave of new members to be admitted. In an attempt to console and to reassure themselves, the Baltic states gradually are shifting to the view that EU membership will in effect extend a Western defence and security umbrella over them as well. To some extent that is true, but it does not carry the ironclad commitment provided by NATO. Still, the Baltic states now hope, too, that membership in the EU and other European organisations will serve them in the longer term as a back door into NATO.

Romania, Bulgaria and Slovenia also continue undauntedly to harbour hopes of NATO membership. In terms of democratisation and economic reforms, Slovenia, which is also among the new members to be admitted by the EU, would be eligible, even though its military contributions would be negligible. But, then, so is Luxembourg's – not to mention Iceland, which has no military forces at all. But sitting next to Croatia, which remains unstable as a result of the collapse of the former Yugoslavia, is seen in NATO as a disadvantage. However, Slovenia's prospects are reasonably good for finding itself inside NATO in the longer term. Romania and Bulgaria are much more difficult cases. While democratisation to some extent has occurred in each, serious political instability reigns in both, and their economic reforms have been minimal. They are also tainted with the brush of the Balkans. 'But we are not part of the Balkans', protested an exasperated Romanian diplomat. This is true by a strict, abstract academic definition of its geography; but the actuality – and its perception in the West – speaks otherwise.

What NATO has done, obviously to appease these aspirant but disappointed countries, is to include them in Partnership for Peace (PfP) and the recently created Euro-Atlantic Partnership Council (EAPC), formerly known as the North Atlantic Co-operation Council, established in 1991, with the Baltic states among its founders. But neither of these provides a security umbrella or the exclusivity of NATO. For not only does Belarus but also the Central Asian republics belong to both PfP and EAPC.

At the Madrid summit, France and Italy pressed strongly, in their own perceived interests, for the admission of Romania and Slovenia in the first 'round'. Indeed, they preferred that to accepting the three Central Europeans as new members. They both feared that the entry of the three Central European countries would shift the alliance's centre of gravity eastwards, and they wished to prevent that by adding a southward extension, a position that Paris and Rome continue to hold. They also staunchly supported Romania's inclusion because of its Latinate character and long historical relationship with them, particularly with France. Denmark was the main and most vocal opponent of the Baltic states' simultaneous inclusion, again to counter the eastward thrust by a northern enlargement as well. Neither found favour with the alliance's majority. But it did lead to the compromise wording of the summit communiqué, leaving the door open, supported by the US to soothe its conscience toward the Baltic states in particular. Another reason for the 'open door' wording was to avoid internal instability among the aspirant countries as a result of their exclusion from the first 'round'. France and Italy were reluctantly ready to include Bulgaria among the first entrants as a matter of contiguity and to strengthen, as they saw it, NATO's 'southern dimension'.

Romania, Bulgaria and Slovenia continue to insist that their inclusion in NATO would strengthen the alliance's southern flank and expand its influence, not least by consolidating its position on the northern shore of the Black Sea. Slovenia argues as well that its admission would ensure the alliance's contiguity by geographically linking Italy with Hungary. They claim with considerable vehemence that their admission would make eminent strategic sense by strengthening NATO's position *vis-à-vis* Russia and also enhancing the alliance's capacity and capability to fend off Islamic extremist penetration into Europe. Playing on NATO members' fears of Islamic extremism is a clever ploy, even if so far an unsuccessful one.

The Baltic states, perhaps even more dismayed than Romania, Bulgaria and Slovenia at being left out of the first 'round', continue to insist that their acceptance into NATO would only strengthen the alliance. Apart from their Europeanness, it makes perfect strategic sense, they insist, because it would enhance Europe's security interests in the face of

Russia's present turmoil and the uncertainties inherent in its future. The US–Baltic Charter signed in early 1998 is helpful but no substitute for NATO protection, they argue. Indeed, they see it for what it essentially is, a palliative.

Among nations presently aspiring to NATO membership, Slovenia stands the best chance in a second 'round', given its basic political stability, its economic condition (even if in need of further reforms), its size and its geographical situation. Romania and Bulgaria are another matter.

After Nicolae Ceausescu's death, Romania's political and economic systems remained on the whole unchanged until 1996, when a new and reformist government came into being. But it has been largely hamstrung by resistance to change within its parliament and bureaucracy, and from massive and widespread corruption in the public and private sectors. Although some political and economic reforms have been put in place, they are very far from completion. Altogether, Romania's political and economic situation is precarious, and the same applies to Bulgaria. But if Romania is admitted, Bulgaria cannot be left out; however, their internal conditions rule out their admission for the foreseeable future.

There is also another important consideration. If Romania and Bulgaria are accepted, denial of the same privilege to the Baltics would be virtually impossible, especially as their internal political and economic circumstances already make them eligible. Denial would undermine their stability because they would see their continued exclusion as a blatant Western betrayal representing NATO's capitulation to Russia. Therefore, as the Baltics are kept out for the foreseeable future because of the Russian element in the equation, it is difficult to see Romania and Bulgaria being admitted even if – and it is a huge question-mark – they eventually implement all requisite political and economic reforms. And while Russia would reluctantly, and after tough political and diplomatic rearguard action, accept Romania's and Bulgaria's entry into NATO, the Baltic republics' admission would result in a political crisis with Moscow, for which the West has already amply shown it has no appetite.

Macedonia, Albania and Slovakia have also expressed an ardent wish to join NATO, but their chances are nil for the foreseeable future. Their argument for their acceptance is basically the same as of the other aspirants. And while their admission would create contiguity, their internal political and economic conditions firmly rule them out. Macedonia is at best unstable because its large Albanian and smaller Serb minorities are deeply influenced by the situation in Albania and Kosovo, as well as by virulent nationalism in Serbia. Albania remains in turmoil and is an economic cripple. Slovakia shows no real signs of shedding, despite occasional but feeble opposition attempts, its neo-Communist dictatorship. NATO's admission of the three new members makes sense for the West's interests, in addition to their own self-interest. It will help stabilise Central Europe by diminishing its fear of Germany and Russia, and thus reduce its acute sense of insecurity. As a concomitant, it will also considerably diminish the risks of incipient nationalist extremism, a sentiment to which the region has traditionally been particularly vulnerable. The favourite argument of these countries' ultra-nationalist element has traditionally been that they are confronted by enemies and betrayed by friends. In the past this line, because it had enough truth in it, succeeded in whipping up embittered zeal, effectively destabilising the region. There is no reason to think that, given the opportunity, the ultra-nationalists will not resort again to this line of agitation. After all, it worked well in the past, and might do so again. It is patently in the security interest of Central Europe and the West as a whole to prevent such instability. That, in fact, is an argument that can be well used with Russia. After all, stability in Central Europe is also in Moscow's self-interest. Not that it would weaken the age-old Russian desire to control the region or at least to be the predominant influence there, a desire stemming from Russia's own profound, traditional sense of insecurity, suspicion and fear of the West.

To be sure, the same argument can validly be made regarding Romania's and Bulgaria's admission. The vital difference is that their internal situations, including their minority problems, still vastly outweigh the advantages of their acceptance into NATO; and this is a situation that shows no foreseeable promise of change.

Of course, the admission of the three Central European states will create new problems inside NATO. It will be difficult for the 'old' members to adjust to a larger, more diverse organisation. Among other things, decision-making will be more complicated, not least because NATO will acquire a new region with its own political and strategic characteristics and interests, which the 'old' members will have to consider on the same terms as they do their own. For their part, the new members, still feeling insecure in their recent independence from Russia, may occasionally exaggerate Russia's potential as a threat. Also, like the other regions of NATO, they will periodically ascribe greater weight to their area than the others are prepared to grant.

At the same time, the Central Europeans will also be inclined to be obdurately and loudly assertive – sometimes even provocative – towards

Russia. This will be true especially of Poland, which is already showing signs of it. The Poles have never muted their traditional, passionate antagonism towards Russia. The other Central and South Central Europeans and Baltic states share this sentiment. But, except for the Baltic states, they tend publicly to be more circumspect, more crafty. The Poles are also keenly aware of being the largest and strategically the most important of the former Soviet satellites. Consequently, they nowadays display a touch of cockiness as a result of the Soviet collapse. They will also vehemently oppose anything that smacks of increased Russian influence on NATO, because they will regard it as a weakening of the alliance, and therefore of their security. They will certainly have nothing to do with the notion of Russia's inclusion in NATO even in the long term. As NATO presumably will continue to require unanimity in its decisions, the Central European trio will automatically possess veto rights. Of course, they will – as other members do – bend under the pressure of the larger NATO nations, but not without a fight inside NATO councils. Once again, Poland will carry considerable weight in arguing its case, which the other two Central European countries will often share, because it will rank among the alliance's larger countries. It is already emboldened by Germany's eagerness to appease it and by the special sense of obligation that Britain, America and France feel towards it, all arising from the history of the Second World War. For its part, the US is influenced as well by domestic political considerations, not least its large electoral constituency of Polish origin.

Significantly, three hardy European neutrals, Finland, Sweden and Austria, are also casting interested eyes at NATO. During the Cold War, Finland adopted a wise and pragmatic policy, dictated by its remote, isolated geography and small population. It is a European country in every sense. But situated next to the Soviet giant and having suffered grievously at its hands during the Finnish–Soviet War in 1939 and the Second World War, Finland chose carefully calibrated neutrality in 1945. Grossly unfair as it was, the West's term for Finland's relationship to the Soviet Union, 'Finlandisation', with its roots in Finland's neutrality, became a pejorative. Finland never had any doubt as to where it belonged. But it had also learnt through its painful history that it could not depend on Western assistance for its defence. At Soviet insistence, Austria was required to adopt neutrality by the State Treaty of 1955 in order to regain its independence and end its occupation by the victorious Four Powers after the Second World War. Since the Napoleonic Wars, Sweden has chosen, as a matter of pragmatism, to pursue neutrality, to its considerable benefit. Not surprisingly, after the end of the Cold

War and the collapse of the Soviet Union, the three began to review their positions. As a result, they joined the EU and are, to varying degrees, looking with interest at NATO membership prospects as well.

Finland is cautiously taking a position of being ready for NATO membership, but only in the longer term. 'Why irritate the bear next door unnecessarily?' remarked a senior Finnish diplomat. 'Otherwise we would join like a shot.' The Swedes are debating the question of joining as a matter of practical sense. The Austrians equally show interest. What gives each added impetus is that the new special relationship between NATO and Russia could well mean that key European security issues directly affecting them would be settled without their involvement. As they see it, their membership in Partnership for Peace and the Euro-Atlantic Partnership Council in this regard is insufficient. However, paradoxically, a deterioration of Moscow's ties with the West might reinforce, for the same reasons as before, Finland's neutrality, yet spur Austria and possibly Sweden to divest themselves of theirs.

There is no opposition within NATO to the admission of Austria and Sweden. The unanimous view is that their membership would enhance NATO by any measure. In fact, NATO would have been delighted to have them inside its portals during the Cold War, if their interests and commitments had permitted it. Finland is another matter. Bordering on Russia, Finland in NATO's eyes is in much the same sensitive position as the Baltic republics. No wonder then that NATO is quietly relieved that Finland voluntarily pursues a policy of showing no overt interest in membership now.

Were Austria to join NATO, a geographical anomaly would be solved. At present, Hungary is in effect an island as a NATO member. With Austria inside NATO, contiguity will be restored. Once Slovenia joins, because of its shared borders with Hungary as well as Austria and Italy, NATO's geographical unity in Europe will be re-established. However, if Slovenia joins first, Austria might choose to stay out, at least for a while, because all its borders except the Slovakian would be with NATO states; thus offering the Austrians continued effective protection without reciprocal commitment or cost. By staying out of the alliance, however, Austria would have no say in NATO decisions affecting its security. Therefore, on balance, Austria would benefit from membership, as would NATO. Similarly, but in the Scandinavian context, Sweden's accession would also be of distinct mutual benefit politically, geographically and therefore strategically.

The actual cost of the presently agreed enlargement is unclear. Estimates range from $1.5 billion to $110 billion over a 10-to-15-year period. A Pentagon study puts it at $27 billion to $35 billion.[4] A Rand Corporation report sets $42 billion as a plausible estimate.[5] The reason why a firm figure is unknowable at this point is that it depends on how much the members, including the new ones, are prepared to pay. The new members, at minimum, have to adjust not only their military doctrine and training but also their command, control and communications systems and their personnel to NATO formats and standards. However, their military equipment, inevitably, is mainly Soviet-made. The question is how rapidly and how extensively it will be desirable – or, indeed, necessary – for them to modernise their gear. The answer is not yet clear. Nor have present members decided yet to what extent, if any, they will help finance the new members' adjustment costs.

Should NATO be enlarged at all, and should the new admissions of 1999 be just the first wave? The answer is yes and a qualified no. The countries designated to enter the alliance are without doubt a part of Europe. They are genuinely democratic, their economies largely reconstructed, their geographical location strategic. On balance, they will add to the alliance by enhancing European stability. The only other countries that should be admitted, for the same reason, are Austria, Slovenia, Sweden and Finland. They, too, qualify by the standards applied to the three Central European countries and they would restore NATO's geographical coherence; but enlargement beyond that would tip the balance against NATO's interests. If the alliance is to be true to its charter, it must remain, above all, a defensive organisation. To be effective, it must be cohesive and coherent. While the Baltic states' Europeanness is beyond question, their vulnerable and difficult geographical position for NATO purposes precludes their admission for the foreseeable future, a condition that is unlikely to change even in the longer term.

With 19 members, NATO's coherence and cohesiveness have occasionally been difficult to sustain, most recently demonstrated during the Balkan crisis. With 23 nations in the alliance, if the three neutrals and Slovenia are eventually admitted, it will be even more difficult, and may have reached the limits of effectiveness. The Organisation for Security and Co-operation in Europe (OSCE), with its large assemblage of members, many of whom cannot by any normal measure be considered as European, is a prime example of unwieldiness and ineffectiveness.

In addition to cohesiveness of purpose and coherence of action, there are other considerations as well. As it is, NATO already has more than enough internal problems, such as the perennial conflict between Turkey and Greece over Cyprus, and faces various other political and social issues. By extending farther east than so far decided, the alliance would automatically inherit an array of bitter border disputes, and virulent national minority and religious problems. NATO's very success over half a century is owed to its coherence and cohesiveness, which have given it a credible deterrence capability (if not credited by everyone in Yugoslavia). The US position of leaving the door open to Russia's membership, strongly opposed by the Western and Central Europeans, is patently verging on the absurd. For not only would it mean NATO's Article 5 responsibilities extending to Russia's borders with the turbulent Central Asian countries, with their large Russian minorities, but also to China. NATO would automatically acquire Russia's severe internal problems in its own Asian republics, such as Chechnya and Dagestan, and rising fundamentalism among its Muslim population. Moreover, unable to dominate the alliance, Russia beyond doubt would do its best to neutralise the alliance's effectiveness, because of its historically inherent fear of the West. Being inside NATO would strengthen Russia's already existing implicit veto by making it explicit. The present American Administration's position, it can only be hoped, is a palliative to Russia, a political ploy rather than a genuine intention. In any case, Russia's admission, as any other country's, would require unanimous assent, including ratification by each NATO member's legislature. Clearly, neither would be forthcoming.

If for no other reason than allowing itself time to digest the absorption of the three new Central European members, NATO should pause for a reasonable period before taking further steps on the question of a second 'wave' of enlargement. Such a planned delay would permit a second stage of expansion to be a tidy affair, with time for all concerned to come to well-considered conclusions. That would, of course, also enhance NATO's cohesion and viability. It is especially needed in view of the pressures and movements in relationships caused by the deepening of the Balkan crisis.

All present signs point to NATO itself wishing to pause now, to digest the absorption of the three new members into its institutions. Thus, there is no serious talk in private, let alone in public, about a timetable for further enlargement. A second 'round' would of course also need the agreement of the three new members, thus ratification by 19 national legislatures. While none of the three new members object to Slovenia's or the neutrals' admission, only Hungary, France and Italy champion Romania's entry (with Germany in support), in an effort to buttress their mutual ties, but even Budapest is cool towards the inclusion of Bulgaria.

Whatever digressions NATO may occasionally make into other spheres, the principal reason for its existence as a defensive organisation should remain unchanged. Without that primarily defensive mission, NATO loses its essential value to the allies, which has served them supremely well for 50 years. Although the Cold War is over, there is more than enough instability around NATO's periphery to warrant the alliance's continued vigilance and viability for its originally intended purpose. Any greater enlargement in size and scope than the 'second wave' now contemplated (Slovenia and possibly the three neutrals) will mean the exact opposite: dilution resulting in ineffectiveness.

Notes

1 Christopher Bobinski, 'Poland advances towards NATO on a broad front', *Financial Times*, 27 June 1997.
2 Henry Kissinger, 'New NATO chips at keystone of US policy', *Daily Telegraph*, 11 April 1997.
3 Ibid.
4 'NATO – the price of expansion', *The Economist*, 15 November 1997.
5 'Cost Studies So Far', *The Military Balance 1997/98* (London: International Institute for Strategic Studies), pp. 269–70.

3

The Future of NATO and the Transatlantic Alliance in the Twenty-First Century

Geoffrey Lee Williams

Introduction

This analysis is divided into a number of inter-related parts. One part concerns the nature of the international order as well as the nature of the future strategic environment. Indeed, we are dealing with a seamless robe whose constituent parts could pre-determine the nature of both NATO and the transatlantic relationship well into the twenty-first century. I therefore will start by discussing the impact of three powerful, simultaneous and intersecting revolutions on international politics. This should enable us to identify the driving forces, predetermined elements and critical uncertainties which, taken together, will shape the future of NATO and the transatlantic alliance which surely has been the most successful security community in twentieth-century history.

The political revolution

I start with the political revolution. This involves looking at the whole structure of world politics wrought by the Second World War, including the end of colonialism and the collapse of the Cold War. The Second World War saw the defeat of Germany, Japan and Italy and the rise of the two superpowers, America and the Soviet Union. It also saw the eclipse of Great Britain as a great power (a former superpower in the nineteenth century) as both world wars took their toll of British resources and capacity for world leadership. France too went into decline.

The end of colonialism

The end of European colonialism contributed to a quantum jump in the number of states, which led to the doubling in size of UN members in ten short years. Likewise, the end of the Cold War saw the rise – though on a more modest scale – of the number of nation-states operating within the international system, with UN membership rising to more than 184 states. This time though, the proliferation of nation-states was accompanied, or rather preceded, by an explosion of non-state actors against the background of a rising tide of ethnicity and extreme nationalism.

Today the claim to self-determination is considered more important than earlier considerations of territorial integrity or of state sovereignty. Thousands of international institutions, non-governmental actors and transnational entities comprise the constituent elements of the international system. For example, in 1970, there were about 7000 multinational companies. In 1998 there were more than 37 000.[1]

Complex interdependence

This explosion in the number of actors has led to the growth of a complex interdependence within the international system, which has eroded the sovereignty of even the most powerful nations on earth. The results have been dramatic. The post-Cold War era is inherently unstable and the system of nation-states is now in a 'Hobbesian' state of nature. We are enveloped by a multiplicity of actors employing a variety of means in pursuit of their goals, involving thousands upon thousands of interactions ebbing and flowing each day in a tidal wave of spontaneous transactions beyond state regulation and control. Risks to individual security at local, regional, national and global levels are inextricably interlocking. From terrorism to high-intensity military campaigns fought with 'smart' as opposed to 'dumb' weapons systems – precision-guided munitions and laser-guided weapons like, for example, the cruise missile are the weapons systems of the future – even political terrorists are becoming more high-tech.[2]

Global threats and new arrangements

There are few threats, then, to security, which despite small beginnings, may not become universal sooner or later. Seen from this global perspective, the earth is now a strategic enclosure in which the ancient issues of security (such as antagonism between the developed and developing, among the armed and arming, between the economically powerful and the poor) cannot be divorced from the postmodern crises of environmental instability, demographic imbalance and resource pressure. Humanity may face common risks in the strategic enclosure; however, universal solutions, while seductive in theory, are illusive in practice. Threats to global security are unlikely to be met with global consensus, and 'spaceship earth' imagery implying shared predicaments and inviting common solutions in an 'interdependent world' are uselessly utopian.

Indeed the post-Cold War era is more an arrangement of *suburbs, precincts,* and *ghettos* with 'winners' and 'losers', as Paul Kennedy emphasises in his book about the prospects in the twenty-first century.[3] The 'losers' range from those in immediate danger from famine or war to all of us, in the long term faced with environmental disasters, economic decline and social malaise.

No solutions yet

We should note that the traditional conviction of the progressive left – namely that there must be solutions – may not survive the test of the new security challenges, many of which are insoluble. The configuration of the international system of the bipolar period of the distribution of power can no longer be sustained. Today, we are split into *suburbs, precincts,* and *ghettos* rather than into the ideologically correct *First, Second* and *Third Worlds* of the Cold War era. Who belongs to whom?

The suburbs

The *suburbs* consist of the powerhouses of Western Europe, North America and the Pacific. They are still comfortable but increasingly uneasy and insecure, clearly not immune from the problems of the precincts and ghettos (which can escalate and spread), nor from the consequences of the environmental instability for which they have some responsibility.

The precincts

The *precincts* include the statelets of Eastern Europe and the Commonwealth of Independent States (CIS) in which development is hampered by social conflict as well as precarious government and ill-developed administrative structures. Living at the heart of the precincts are the Middle East oil-producers and the East Asian industrialising economies. By definition, dangers and growing risks in the developing precincts have implications for those residing in the *suburbs* whose willingness to intervene in the turbulence of the precincts becomes a major source of tension between them.

I expect deep rifts between the powerhouse(s) and hegemon(s) whose own predominance is under possible threat due to domestic politics, economic strain and poor or mediocre leadership. Thus, disparate tendencies could split the European–American partnership, arising from the clash between wealthy suburban states which have taken no global responsibilities (say, Germany or Japan) and those countries like Britain and France who are willing to apply military force out-of-area in support of UN, OSCE or NATO mandates. Finally, we must turn to consider the position of the *ghettos*.

The ghettos

The *ghettos* of international politics are to be found in parts of what is still called, somewhat misleadingly, 'the Third World'. This area suffers from ever-greater noise and disturbance than the more unstable parts of the precincts. Why? Because of the ever-greater damage inflicted on the environment caused by resource pressure, diminishing quality and quantity of resources and the ever-present population pressure adding to the damage sustained to the eco-system. Disease and migration will become major factors inducing deep malaise and alienation in the extremes of the ghettos, or violent unrest on a grand scale.

The coming chaos

It is to be expected that much conflict will arise from the consequences of cultural antagonism to change. Even sections of the suburbs and precincts may resist globalisation. In the ghettos especially, traditional belief systems regarding fertility, ancestry and the role of the family (in Africa in particular) will run up against pressures produced by attempts to modernise and democratise economic and political entities.

To sum up, the strategic environment will be both politically violent and unstable. Thus, the strategic environment remains the most crucial and salient factor affecting the decision to acquire nuclear, chemical and bacteriological weapons by nation-states still living in a state of nature despite the hopeful atmosphere generated by the end of the Cold War.

We must expect the next decade or so, in which American power and will are under extreme pressure, to be chaotic and turbulent, while Europe is assailed by nationalism and the spectre of mass migration.[4]

The process of European integration will slow down in the short term in the face of intractable problems associated with the merger of political systems, the merger of governmental systems, the merger of economic systems, the merger of peoples and societies and the removal of state boundaries. In Europe, then, there is a real danger of fragmentation in both NATO and the EU whose activities lie at the heart of *suburbia* or what we used to call the West.

Both Europe and America will face a multiplicity of missile threats of different ranges and warheads over the next decade. These missile systems will be in the hands of precinct countries, reflecting the new axis of global conflict; the North–South conflict thus replacing the recent East–West divide. The manifest dangers arising from radical nationalism, ethnic strife and religious fundamentalism will affect Europe as well as other parts of the globe.

Of course, Japan and China will emerge as military hegemons to match their economic dominance of Asia – one already in suburbia and the other still in the precincts – while the population explosion in Africa and Asia will precipitate new global dangers. It is time now to turn to the second part of my trilogy of revolutions, concerning science and technology.

The scientific and technological revolution

I now turn to the second revolution in human affairs, the scientific and technological revolution, which has expanded man's mastery of his environment with greater speed in every decade. The evidence of this confronts us almost every month. The revolution in military technology since, and indeed before, the end of the Second World War saw the dramatic development of nuclear weapons, space technology and electronics. These revolutions in military technologies triggered a secondary wave of innovation with the development in microelectronics, telecommunications and computer technology. This in turn wrought the information revolution, the information super-highways. These technologies and scientific achievements, like their predecessors, have transformed the nature of warfare. In this century alone, there have been several revolutionary waves whose impact has been such that we can, from this vantage point, briefly describe them, if only to see where military science is heading.[5]

The meaning for NATO

The implications for the future of NATO are obvious in the field of military science. Clearly, the attrition warfare of 1914–18 was replaced by mechanised warfare based on developments in the 1920s and 1930s which matured in time for the Second World War. This was made possible by developments in aircraft design, radio, radar, and, of course, advances in the internal combustion engine. Preparations for the Third World War, the period of the Cold War, lay in the further exploitation of nuclear weapons and ballistic missiles. Their full development came too late to affect the outcome of the Second World War, but, in its final stages, the advent of atomic bombs, the V-1 cruise-missile and the V-2 ballistic missile foreshadowed the nature of future conflict.

Today, we stand at the threshold of new ways of fighting or determining wars through cybernetics and automated troop control. These developments are pregnant with possibilities, not least of which is the impact they will have on the balance between *attrition* and *manoeuvre* in warfare. Many believe that the emerging military revolution (EMR) elevates information above both weapons of attrition and manoeuvre, thus allowing them to be applied with sensationally accurate results. This will be a military revolution characterised by the ubiquitous employment of microprocessors throughout military force structures. The technology feeding this revolution does not destroy anything *per se* nor indeed transport physical objects such as troops and equipment over vast distances. Rather, it permits the precise application of pure force against an enemy's vital centres of gravity, and it supports the assembly and deployment of forces in space and time so as to maximise their operational impact and minimise their own vulnerability.[6]

In brief, this means that both NATO and its guiding superpower, the USA, must better develop and deploy this technology in order to deal with the different types of conflicts likely to arise in the future. Fortunately, the United States appears to understand this.

The economic and industrial revolution

Turning finally to the economic and industrial revolution, I will be brief. We know how rapid is the pace of innovation in every aspect of our material life, in communications, transport, building and education; but, as we have noted above, nowhere has it been made more hectic than in the military sciences. The reason is that the industrial powers spend record amounts of money on military research and development. This is about 100 times as much in real terms as they spent before 1939. Spending by the early 1960s probably exceeded four times what they were spending at the height of the Second World War. A new industrial and economic revolution was well underway even before the Cold War reached its zenith. It is worth recalling that many on the British left, including Richard Crossman, were predicting that the planned economies of the Soviet Union and those of its satellites in Central and Eastern Europe would produce even more spectacular results than their capitalist counterparts whose economies lacked proper planning mechanisms. Few, then, would have predicted the collapse of central planning and the demise of the socialist command economies and their bloated communist political systems.

Yet, the triumph of the open society and its economy was not and is not inevitable. But, as we approach the turn of the century, we certainly are entitled to be optimistic about the future of capitalist democracy. The global economy is a fact: worldwide markets have been opened up to competition as trade volumes reach new heights.

The US ascendant in a multipolar world

Although the bipolar world is giving way to a multipolar one, it is clear that the US still retains its economic, scientific and technological ascendancy. It is the driving force behind such initiatives as the US and EU Transatlantic Declaration of 1990 and the follow-up New Transatlantic Agenda signed in 1995.[7] Despite the dramatic growth of the world economy since 1945 when the US accounted for 85 per cent of world output, the American economy today is more than *twice* the size of its nearest competitor and, in contrast to the European Union for example, it also enjoys low inflation, low unemployment and tremendous growth.

America still rejects a complete return to isolationism, and, indeed, openly espouses an enlarged NATO, a revitalised Euro-American partnership and a transatlantic free trade area (TAFTA). The classic conditions for a neo-Atlantic partnership might then flower in the future instead of the historic Europeanist alternative with its protectionist and corporatist overtones.[8] A real choice has to be made. It is time now to turn to the European dimension of political, economic and strategic change before returning to the subject of the future of the transatlantic relationship and NATO.

The European dimension

I start with a general point before turning to the detail. Were the size of the European Union (EU) to increase to 25 countries and beyond, it would mark, in my judgement, the emergence of a wider and essentially non-federal Europe with an inner core of 'federated' states possessing a single currency and a common macro-economic policy. Clearly, this enlargement of the EU would prove to be even more problematic than the expansion of NATO (itself certain to expand beyond the recently admitted Visegrad three – Poland, Hungary and the Czech Republic). A second wave of new members is likely, consisting of Romania and Slovenia, to be followed in the fullness of time by a third wave comprising Slovakia, Albania, Bulgaria and Macedonia. Then, a possible fourth wave embracing Estonia, Latvia, Lithuania and Croatia might appear, and be followed by a final wave of former neutrals: Sweden, Finland, Austria and the Irish Republic. Thus, by 2020, say, NATO would have expanded from 16 to 28 members in 20 years! Given this prospect, it would help our analysis if we began to define the difference between *security* and *defence* in the European situation, and thus proceeded to explore the difficulties faced in combining nations' efforts into *collective security* and *collective defence*.[9]

Definition of collective security and defence

The disappearance of a massive unidirectional threat has refocused European minds on the appearance of less precise or predictable risks with potential for escalation and spillover. Consequently, the definition of *security* is broadening after having a very narrow focus during the period of the Cold War. The term, 'security', being so widely and literally interpreted, deserves some clarification. In its current, all-embracing sense, it is a product of the twentieth century, being used in this form to describe past aspirations for 'collective security' through the League of Nations and the United Nations.[10]

Security can be defined as attempts to resolve conflicts that might endanger peace, and *defence* as any deterrent or retaliatory action by countries to secure their territorial integrity and protect their vital interests. Yet, it would, of course, be overly simplistic to claim that defence begins when security has failed. Defensive tasks typically take place concurrently with security, such as the building of air-defence infrastructures, pre-positioning of forces and the maintenance of nuclear deterrence. It is unhelpful and contentious to compose an exhaustive list of the elements that go to make up security, as they will vary with circumstances.

The case of European security

In the case of European security in the last few years of the twentieth century, the definition must include (but not be limited to) territorial integrity, the functioning of the national economy, safeguards against subversion and the preservation of international peace. Also, European security must be pursued by a combination of diplomatic, military and economic means. The challenges to Europe's future fall broadly into two categories: 'hard' security and 'soft' security. 'Hard' security issues are characterised by external armed attack against the land mass or the threat of mass destruction and are broadly issues of defence. Soft security issues form 'lower-level' threats including the collapse of democratic forms of government, international organised crime, mass migration, poverty and social problems around the European perimeter and dependence on raw materials.

Collective defence or collective security

The differences between *defence* and *security* are important to many arguments, and any blurring of the distinction between the two can be critical, particularly in the context of collective defence or collective security. In political terms, agreement on collective defence is relatively easy to achieve, as defence is much closer to being an absolute quantity than security. Sovereign nations can readily agree on the existence of an armed threat to their territorial integrity, and on the need and methods to counter that threat. The history of NATO between 1949 and 1989 demonstrated this in practice. Indeed, defence cooperation has collateral political advantage in providing a cohesive factor for all the involved nations and their political parties. On the other hand, security is a less easily defined concept and is capable of differing interpretations.

Attempts to achieve collective security can easily fragment an alliance, whereas collective defence has a bonding effect. Surely a current example would be the differing perceptions concerning the security imperative as seen by the US determination to maintain trade sanctions against Cuba against the wishes of the European powers who want normal trading relations. Contrast this disunity with the situation in 1962 when the Soviet Union started deploying nuclear ballistic missiles in Cuba. This was seen as a clear-cut defence issue and consequently US action attracted broad support. In terms of hard security (or defence), Europe has few immediate problems. The threat of a massive short-notice conventional attack from the East has receded to a very long-term potential that would need years of preparation to bring to fruition.

Although the states which border Europe to the south and south-east pose security problems, they have no capability to invade Europe, although Turkey could conceivably face attack from her Middle Eastern neighbours. Of course, NATO or EU expansion eastward beyond the Visegrad three could bring new challenges.[11]

Defence is therefore an issue that is increasingly taking a back seat as the Cold War becomes a distant memory. Consequently, there is a greater squeeze on defence budgets, leading to smaller, less capable defence forces. At first sight, this is a reasonable response and one would have to question either the government's intention or the political accountability of any national force that did not shrink as its *raison d'être* declined.

Nevertheless, the tools of defence are almost exactly the same tools as used for security, particularly when the Western trend in security operations is to use overwhelming force to minimise casualties, 'the sledgehammer to crack a nut'. These lower levels of armed forces will soon affect the West's capability to deploy forces for missions that are not vital to national survival but are, nevertheless, important to regional stability. Europe, largely due to its anarchic history, faces considerable problems of 'soft' security. These range from the uncertain stability of newly democratic states in Central and Eastern Europe, through territorial and ethnic disputes that are the legacy of centuries of conflict, to dangers of mass migration and the instability on Europe's southern and southeastern flanks.

In the main, security risks are not military but political and economic. However, military means do have a role and offer at least a partial answer to many nations' concerns about the stability of their new democratic institutions. They wish to lock themselves into the major alliances of the West, including the military institutions of NATO and the Western European Union (WEU).

Why has NATO survived?

Despite the realisation that NATO had been deprived of an enemy with the collapse of the Soviet Union in 1991, the early optimism about the end of conflict in Europe was soon dashed by the bloody break-up of Yugoslavia. This tragic event was, of course, preceded by Iraq's invasion of Kuwait, an event which disproved the thesis that war in the old sense was obsolete.

These two interrelated crises brought NATO back to centre stage, though in the case of Bosnia, it threatened to split the alliance irrevocably. NATO's air strikes against Serb positions and coordinated ground action in August/September 1995 transformed the situation. The NATO-led operation was quickly followed by the American inspired Dayton peace accords which led to the formation of the peace implementation force (IFOR), which, in its turn, was superseded by the creation of a stabilisation force (SFOR) in 1997–98 (now DFOR). Of course, the military side was stunningly successful, but the political scenario still remains unclear at the time of writing.[12] However, both IFOR and SFOR, like the earlier NATO-led Operation Desert Storm, backed by American military power, gave NATO a new lease of life and its future seemed reasonably assured.

This impression was reinforced by the relative and absolute failure of the European Union's peace efforts in Bosnia, which revealed how ill-prepared it was to implement the successful common foreign and security policy (CFSP) envisaged in the Maastricht Treaty. It could not manage the crisis without NATO; that is, the United States.

The transformation of NATO

NATO achieved a radical reform programme, which saw it transformed into an effective post-Cold War alliance. The North Atlantic Co-operation Council (NACC), Partnership for Peace (PfP) and the concept of combined joint task forces (CJTF) were all the prelude to further innovation which, by the high summer of 1997, saw NATO agree to add three new members to the alliance by 1999. The NACC was transformed into the Euro-Atlantic Partnership Council (EAPC) and the PfP programme was enhanced (PfP2 or PfP+) in order to expand cooperation with those nations participating in its work. Thus NATO reformed itself but stuck, in principle, to a collective defence model rather than seeking a looser collective security role, along the lines of the pan-European OSCE model.[13]

However, the issue of the further expansion of NATO does raise critical questions about the continued validity of the Article 5 obligation of the Washington Treaty (which envisages that an attack on one is an attack on all). This may lack credibility within a larger alliance. NATO's future, like its past, rests on its credibility as a military alliance, and central to this is the continued existence of the transatlantic alliance. This in turn must rest upon a Europeanised NATO, developed under the rubric of a European Security and Defence Identity (ESDI), working with but not being subordinate to the Western European Union.[14]

The transatlantic alliance: the neo-Atlanticist dimension

The early geopoliticians, notably Captain Alfred Thayer Mahan and Sir Halford Mackinder, leaving to one side extreme German theorists, introduced the concept of the European Heartland, control of which gave mastery of Eurasia and engendered conflict with the Rimland controlled by the sea powers. It was Germany's continuing purpose throughout the early part of this century to wrest control of the Heartland from Russia and control both the Rimland and Heartland, thus becoming an overwhelming hegemonic power.

Only a power external to the contest in Europe could muster the economic and military might to prevent continental domination by a single state. The role of external power was exercised by Britain throughout the nineteenth century and by the United States during the twentieth century.

History demonstrates that without a hegemon, Europe is vulnerable to internal pressure and external domination. Only a federal Europe could change this hard truth; however, a European federation, though possible in principle, is unlikely in practice for the foreseeable future. If, therefore, Europe needs an extra-territorial hegemon, who should or can play that role?

Russia, already in control of the Eurasian Heartland, would become too powerful with both Rimland and Heartland under her control, so nations of the Rimland, wary that her hegemony feeds on territorial aggrandisement, would reject her suit. The conclusion is that only America, with no territorial claims in Europe, can presently fulfil the function; but if America should decline to expend the energy and treasure necessary to be the hegemon, where does the natural power in Europe lie?

German domination

The former German chancellor Helmut Kohl believes that an American withdrawal or a collapse of NATO without the precondition of a federal Europe would inevitably thrust Germany, as Europe's most economically successful, populous and central power, into that position. This is a prospect that successive leaders of Germany, apparently including Herr Kohl's successors in power, feel would be historically inadvisable.

For 50 years, the US has made a commitment to European security one of the pillars of its defence. At the height of Soviet military power and ambition, the US forward defence of Europe could reasonably be regarded as vital to Europe's security. However, the end of the Cold War, a consequent resurgence of regional security problems throughout the world and domestic demands for a peace dividend have caused the US to re-evaluate its global security priorities and encourage Europe to bear a greater share of the burden.

Post-Maastricht tension

The 1992 Maastricht Treaty on European Union (TEU) established an EU common foreign and security policy (CFSP) as a mechanism for governments of member nations to coordinate their own foreign and security policies.[15] The CFSP recognised the need by European nations to take more responsibility for their defence within the membership of NATO. Simultaneously, the Western European Union (WEU) was to be developed as a security component of the EU and the European pillar. Yet the reality was so very different, as events were to reveal.

Europe's manifest inability to muster the political cohesion to influence the situation in the Balkans, the EU's own backyard, is given as the *locus classicus*: this merely being the latest in a sequence of events in Europe that could not apparently be resolved without American leadership and military power.[16] There is, however, a growing confidence within European institutions, despite the recent diplomatic failure in the Balkans, that a common European view on foreign and security policy can be found. But can it? The current plan is for the WEU's functions to be transferred to the EU under the secretaryship of Javier Solana, who moves over from being NATO's Secretary-General. The WEU would cease to exist as an institution outside the EU, but for ease of reference I shall continue to refer to the European 'dimension' as the WEU.

Cognitive resources and the realities

There is a kind of cognitive dissonance at work here among European elites, especially if they are German, on the question of European security. Yet it is clear that US involvement remains the prerequisite for European defence and security. Europe's defence capabilities without America are inadequate against a long-term great power threat. The economic and, perhaps more important, social costs of increasing defence capability to rival that of a great-power rival are politically unacceptable to most Europeans.

It is not that the European nations are incapable of producing the military forces to carry out likely security (as opposed to defence) functions, but Europe does not possess enough political cohesion to carry through a security operation that is other than completely uncontentious. The *locus classicus* of this point is the European Union's failure to influence the course of the Bosnian war until American leadership, harnessed through NATO, was available for resolute action. Perhaps Europe will only gain adequate cohesion for an effective security policy when and if it achieves something very close to a federated status. This could be some way off even if it were desirable, which I very much doubt.

The twenty-first century

International order in the twenty-first century will therefore depend upon the United States and a Europeanised NATO, working with but outside any security structures formed by the European Union. The WEU is unlikely to displace NATO as the primary defence body while the United States remains a member of NATO. NATO without America would be a broken reed; the WEU without NATO would be a busted flush. Chaos and confusion would then quickly engulf the whole of Europe.

Yet this outcome is unlikely. NATO serves American interests jointly shared with its European allies, some of whom are also the leading powers in the evolving European Union. The continued existence of the Atlantic alliance does not solely rest on military and strategic convergence between its members. Trade is vital to all: already trade and investment flows cry out for a more structured economic framework. Two-way trade amounts to about $300 billion per year and direct investment totals some $650 billion, reflecting a combined transatlantic output of over $2 trillion. Thus, it would not be too dramatic to say that North America and Europe are at the epicentre of a growing web of transborder investment, technology and ideas. This new artery of the burgeoning global economy rests on solid foundations: about 40 per cent of all US profits earned abroad derive from Western Europe, where US firms have invested some $350 billion or nearly 50 per cent of their total foreign investment. Moreover, three-fifths of all foreign investment in the US is estimated to have come from Western Europe. Europe does not matter any less to America just because Asia's significance has grown; trade is not a zero-sum game.

Can we then, look forward to the future of NATO and the transatlantic alliance in the twenty-first century with growing confidence that strategic and economic interests will continue to converge more than they diverge?

A strategy for the millennium?

NATO has already established the basis for an appropriate strategy for the twenty-first century by recognising that conflict has not come to an end in international politics despite the end of the Cold War and that the WEU and the European Union are not able or willing to displace NATO. NATO has transformed itself as both a defence and a security organisation. Based on the continued relevance of collective defence, NATO remains capable of dealing with the security challenges of the future.

Yet much remains to be done. We need to develop a long-term, comprehensive vision of the transatlantic partnership in a world no longer faced by a common threat. The search for a 'grand new bargain' must address two vital policy issues, concerning which there will be considerable debate. The first issue is the part, if any, NATO should play at the global level in order to give substance to the Euro-Atlantic partnership.

The second issue is how NATO–Europe can contribute to a more *equal* relationship with the United States in military capabilities.

There are three big obstacles which inhibit a 'grand new bargain': America's reluctance to dilute her dominant leadership role; a European culture of dependency that effectively prevents a more mature relationship with the US; and the decline in European military capabilities and its related problem of mobilising popular support for increased defence provision.[17]

The basis for a new partnership, with NATO as its centrepiece, must be centred on the various economic, strategic and regional agendas, which must then be reconciled with the institutional changes occurring in both NATO and the EU. If NATO were to develop a global dimension in its strategic thinking, would this weaken or strengthen the Euro-Atlantic partnership?

The events of 1997 confirm the overwhelming impression that a real global dimension would greatly strengthen NATO in the years that lie ahead. A new, transformed NATO has evolved over the last seven or eight years. The new NATO has delivered on many aspects of its declared intentions, and defined its agenda for years to come at the 1999 Washington conference marking its fiftieth anniversary.

NATO has increased its membership and kept an 'open door' policy concerning future accessions. Even more strikingly, it was decided to replace the old North Atlantic Co-operation Council (NACC) with the new Euro-Atlantic Partnership Council (EAPC), which brings into political orbit former adversaries and the European neutrals.

The Russians have been given, through the NATO–Russian Founding Act a conditional and limited part in formulating European security, without possessing a *de facto* veto over NATO's defence posture or future defence policies. The biggest issue still centres on the idea of a European Security and Defence Identity (ESDI), which implies the future Europeanisation of NATO rather than a conscious effort to expand the role of the WEU and the EU in the area of defence as opposed to security.

With respect to defence, Russia remains the long-term potential threat to Europe. Will the Russian Federation embark upon a virtual reconstruction of a centralised state based on an autocratic system? To put it bluntly, Russia can either be a democracy or an empire; she cannot be both. But she could be neither if the Commonwealth of Independent States (CIS) breaks up into three possible constituent parts: a Slavic bloc, a Ukrainian bloc (with the Baltic states) and a Muslim bloc. Such an outcome might or might not then undermine European security as a whole, but we can easily imagine circumstances where the European Union could find itself with greatly diminished military capabilities, having to deter or defend against threats to its vital interests.

The EU will be unable to sustain a credible defence policy unless and until it is prepared to spend more on defence capabilities, especially if NATO ceases to be effective or the United States withdraws from Europe. A purely European defence effort could prove to be a chimera, unless the three principal European military powers, Britain, France and Germany, were prepared to merge their defence capabilities to form the inner core of a European army. Even then, this would prove a second-best solution to a US-led NATO if Russia were, once again, to become a major threat. As was noted above, Russia remains an enigma. The largest threat comes from instability within society and the economy. There are now some indications of dis-investment, which is truly worrying.

But there are some early signs that Germany is beginning once again to see Russia as a potential ally, within the new power structure emerging in Europe. What is therefore the future relationship of Moscow with Paris and Bonn (the inner core of the EU)? A Franco-German–Russian triangle would tend to put Russia on a par with the Franco-German axis (the locomotive of the EU). Poland has been developing a similar trilateral arrangement, known as the Weimar Triangle, with Paris and Bonn. This suits Germany because such an arrangement could prove to be a useful way of offsetting growing concern that she is turning Central Europe into her strategic and economic *imperium*.

Thus, Germany wants to pass off its bilateral links with Moscow as a Russia–EU link, which, of course, includes the Franco-German partnership. Britain is worried that this sort of thinking precludes British influence in a wider Europe. From a marked British perspective, future choices look invidious. Joining the single currency zone (EMU) is a poor substitute for that wider diplomatic influence which Britain has in NATO (or is seeking in an essentially non-federal Europe). Given the UK's exclusion from the arrangements governing a single currency in the absence of actual British participation in EMU, British influence in Europe must rest on its military contribution to NATO. How to maintain influence on the basis of national power when the Franco-German axis within the EU is pushing towards a fully-fledged federation has become the question of the hour.

Should Britain become the third partner of the Franco-German enclave or seek to build a counteracting balance of power against it, with America as the linchpin in a new transatlantic partnership? Is it already too late to think in such traditional terms? I think not. National interests shape international institutions more than they are shaped by them and the European Union should be no exception to this.[18]

The triumph of intergovernmentalism over supra-nationalism in the realms of defence and even security have been demonstrated by a comparison between NATO and the EU in the light of events since the end of the Cold War. Nation-states are still the most effective actors in both entities, and the federalist logic of the EU has definite limitations once it is challenged by the assertion of national interests. As President de Gaulle once observed, international treaties are like young girls and roses – they last as long as they last. The experiment in merging national currencies will last as long as it lasts.

The future of NATO and the transatlantic alliance rests upon the reconciliation of national interests reached on the basis of trial and error, rather than on the basis that the European nation-state must cede its position to a federal structure seeking to become a superpower.

The first two decades of the twentieth century could see a transformed and expanded NATO, together with a larger hybrid European Union, partly supra-national and partly intergovernmental, underpinning the emergence of a transatlantic free-trade area upon whose economic and scientific strength world peace will largely rest. But let me now turn to consider the future of NATO in relation to the development of the concept of combined joint task forces (CJTFs), which addresses the issues of who does what and why.

Combined joint task forces?

At the January 1994 NATO summit meeting in Brussels, in an initiative designed to provide a more adaptable and flexible way to meet the military demands of the post-Cold War world, leaders approved the Combined Joint Task Force command and control concept. Suggested in 1993 by the United States as a mechanism for meeting the crisis-management and out-of-area needs of the alliance politically and militarily, the CJTFs are essentially, as described by NATO, 'multinational and multi-service formations established for specific contingency operations.'[19]

The concept is intended to provide the alliance with more institutional flexibility in efficiently dealing with situations in and outside of Europe in peacekeeping and contingency operations. While CJTFs can be used within the alliance's border, the concept possibly more importantly also overcomes some of the barriers NATO faced in the search to meet needs beyond its borders, to operate in non-Article 5 situations.[20]

The CJTF concept offers states that are not members of NATO's integrated military structure, particularly Partnership for Peace (PfP) members, an opportunity to act in cooperation with NATO. It also enables the WEU (with the approval of the North Atlantic Council) to undertake operations where NATO decides not to become involved. The idea of a CJTF is not necessarily a new one. Joint task forces (JTFs) involving components from two or more services and combined task forces (CTFs) using forces from two or more countries have been used by both the American and British militaries for some time. Notable examples include the D-Day landings during the Second World War and the military forces used in the Persian Gulf in 1991. What is new about the idea is the permanent institutionalisation, within NATO, of the multinational force concept and its contribution to NATO's operational security.

CJTFs have a significant political value for their function in bridging the divide between NATO and the WEU as well as the divide between the political and the military. The idea is not only about the mechanics of NATO's operational reform. It is also, fundamentally, about maintaining the meaning of the transatlantic link in the new international circumstances.[21] The concept serves to improve cooperation with the WEU and reflect the emerging European Security and Defence Identity (ESDI) by providing 'separable but not separate' military forces that could be employed either by NATO or the WEU.[22] Because of the nature of the operational structure and the potential for WEU-led operations without US participation, CJTFs also serve the function of strengthening the European pillar of the alliance and providing an answer to US calls for more equitable burden- and responsibility-sharing within the alliance.

Definition and structure of CJTF

For military purposes, 'a CJTF can be described as: a multinational, multiservice, task-tailored force consisting of NATO and possibly non-NATO forces capable of rapid deployment to conduct limited duration peace operations beyond Alliance borders, under the control of either NATO's integrated military structure or the WEU'.[23] In addition to humanitarian tasks, CJTFs could also involve participation in a collective defence scenario. All of these operations would most likely be implemented as a result of an Organisation for Security and Co-operation in Europe (OSCE) or United Nations (UN) mandate. The concept also enables the participation of NATO partner countries that are not part of the integrated military structure. The current joint multiservice Bosnian Peace Implementation Force (IFOR) closely resembles what a NATO-led CJTF will look like in practice, and lessons learned there have served as a guide for NATO's CJTF planning staffs.

The concept is promoted as providing the necessary circumstances to encourage the Europeans in defining their ESDI and promote closer European military cooperation. 'In time it should increase Europe's sense of responsibility, leading to a more balanced burden-sharing in NATO and hindering the decline in defence budgets by maintaining an active European role.'[24] CJTFs are intended, in this way, to strengthen the NATO–WEU relationship with the assurance that the organisations are guided by the principles of transparency and complementarity and that there is no duplication of military capabilities and structures.[25]

These conditions serve to ensure that the Atlantic alliance remains the central authority in European security operations with the WEU and the ESDI developing within that body instead of separate from and rival to it. ESDI was approved formally by the NATO foreign ministers at the Berlin Ministerial Meeting in 1996. It includes elements of closer cooperation between NATO and the WEU: joint meetings between the WEU Council and the NAC, case-by-case potential availability of NATO assets to support WEU-led operations, and NATO–WEU consultations on the planning and operation of these missions. Further, NATO will conduct exercises and planning of WEU illustrative missions in cooperation with the WEU, and NATO's defence planning system will take account of WEU-led operations.[26]

From the introduction of the CJTF concept in 1994 to its approval in 1996, the North Atlantic Council (NAC) and the NATO military authorities worked, sometimes with stalled or little progress, on the development and design of the CJTF idea. Approved at the 1996 Berlin Ministerial Meeting, the Overall Politico-Military Framework for the CJTF Concept gives the NAC political control and power of approval (by unanimous vote) over NATO CJTFs. It contains details about the employment and function of CJTFs to assist NATO in performing efficient missions, to direct operations with the participation of non-NATO states, and to encourage the formation of ESDI.[27] It also discusses the structure of CJTFs and provides details about staffing, headquarters and operations.

The CJTF capability does not require additional structure from the organisations involved, only reorganisation within the existing frameworks. This is achieved mainly through the process of 'dual hatting' personnel and positions within existing headquarters. These identified positions and personnel form the CJTF 'nuclei' and provide the central elements of the Combined Joint Task Forces Headquarters (CJTF HQ) to which additional elements will be contributed for operations. These selected elements would perform their daily functions within the

NATO structure, but if a crisis situation arose, they would be removed or 'borrowed' from the central structure by NATO or the WEU to perform in the CJTF capacity.

The three headquarters that so far have been designated as CJTF 'parent headquarters' are Striking Fleet Atlantic (STRIKE-FLTLANT) at Norfolk, Virginia, Allied Forces Central Europe (AFCENT) in Brunssum and Allied Forces Southern Europe (AFSOUTH) in Naples.[28]

The CJTF HQ are responsible for logistic and operational planning and implementation, control and coordination of operations, coordination with participating governments, agencies and forces and monitoring operation progress.[29] CJTF HQ will be capable of quick formation and deployment command of both NATO and non-NATO forces, intelligence coordination, communication with other commands and organisations as well as the ability to be self-sustaining for 30 days. These HQs will have the responsibility of quick response in emergency situations both in and out of area (deployment of the leading elements within seven days), coordination and accommodation of NATO and WEU practices, and the ability to cooperate with non-NATO countries in planning.[30] In the case of a WEU-led operation, the designated CJTF commander, instead of reporting through NATO channels, would come under the direction of the WEU Council of Ministers and report through the command structure of the WEU. If NATO assets are used in a European operation, they will be put under the control of the WEU commander.[31]

Despite a slow start in getting the idea to an operational stage, NATO has recently conducted trial exercises of the CJTF concept using the designated CJTF HQ. Completed in April 1998, the trials were conducted inside other scheduled NATO trials, Allied Effort 97 (AE97) and Strong Resolve 98 (SR98). HQ AFCENT was the parent CJTF HQ for AE97, and

Table 3.1 General structure of a CJTF HQ[32]

Permanent staff elements	Non-permanent staff elements	
CJTF HQ Nucleus	*Augmentation Modules*	*Supporting Modules*
Composed of staff drawn from CJTF parent HQ: • Nucleus Chief • Planning section • Operations section • Intelligence section • Support section • Other sections as applicable.	Resources provided for a specific operation by NATO HQs, other national sources to augment sections in CJTF HQ nucleus.	Resources for additional sections required for a specific operation (e.g. specialised capabilities) provided by NATO HQs or national sources.

STRIKFLTLANT was used as the parent HQ for the sea-based SR98. The Major NATO Commanders (MNC), Supreme Headquarters Allied Powers Europe (SHAPE) and Supreme Allied Commander Atlantic (SACLANT) are drafting a report on the trial exercises which will discuss the MNC recommendations for the further implementation of the concept including the number of CJTF HQs, their location, sustainment and operations. The NATO Military Committee will use the results to make further recommendations for CJTF implementations, and the NAC will have the final approval over these recommendations.[33]

NATO, the WEU and CJTF

The political value of the CJTF concept is nowhere more apparent than in its impact on the WEU and building of the ESDI. It is this arena that is also the most contentious. CJTFs provide the WEU with the potential to command these 'separable but not separate' NATO assets when the alliance chooses not to act in a crisis situation. 'The NAC will approve the release of NATO assets and capabilities for WEU-led operations, keep itself informed on their use through monitoring with the advice of the NATO Military Authorities and through regular consultations with the WEU Council, and keep these under review.'[34]

In other words, with the approval of the NAC, NATO can provide the WEU with a CJTF HQ and other capabilities and assets necessary to support a WEU-led operation. NATO-owned assets like communications systems and the Airborne Warning and Control System (AWACS) can be made available to a coalition of willing Europeans, under WEU command, to carry out an operation in a non-Article 5 situation where the US chooses not to participate. The WEU also has the option of borrowing assets that are earmarked by NATO member states for NATO. In practice, this will probably include American lift and intelligence capabilities. Thus, the separable but not separate concept is a significant one, serving to avoid duplication of capabilities and maintaining a single command structure that provides coherence and effectiveness in alliance capabilities.[35]

Since the Berlin Ministerial Meeting in 1996, the Alliance has been working with the WEU, elaborating procedures and arrangements that would make WEU-led operations possible, and identifying assets and capabilities that could potentially be made available to meet the requirements of a mission that the WEU could envisage itself undertaking. These missions would likely be limited to smaller and limited levels of operation dealing with humanitarian, rescue and peacekeeping tasks and crisis management.[36] Further negotiations regarding the details surrounding NATO asset transfer to the WEU and associated issues like information sharing, leadership positions and operation responsibility and liability are currently taking place within NATO, with political direction from the member states, especially the US.[37]

The United States has asked the WEU to consult NATO first should they contemplate conducting a mission, providing NATO with information about the objectives (military and political) of the operation as well as estimates of what sorts of capabilities their plans might require and a time frame for completion.[38] This requirement is based on the principle that in many cases, if there is a situation in Europe that requires military action, the United States will want to be involved. If the US chooses not to take part in the operation, but approves it, then the WEU will proceed on its own with NATO assets.[39]

There were other points that caused animosity in the concept negotiation, primarily between the United States and France. The antagonism between the two nations over European security has historical roots stemming back to France's withdrawal from NATO's integrated military structure in 1966. After the Cold War, France continued her assertion that the institutions of the European Union could decide their own security policy and that they would no longer need to rely on or accept US involvement or leadership. With the unfolding events in Bosnia and Yugoslavia, however, and European impotence in the situation, the French realised that the United States still had a role to play, even without the Soviet threat. They also realised that ESDI could not sustain itself outside of the alliance at present. These realisations, combined with NATO approval and facilitation of the CJTF and ESDI ideas at the Berlin summit, have served to bring France closer to the Alliance's military structure; but this new-found closeness is not without contentious issues.

One of the central points of negotiation between France and the United States was the manner in which NATO-dedicated assets would be made available for the WEU to borrow. Because, as will be discussed below, the WEU has the capabilities to carry out only very limited operations at present, the majority of the assets supplied for the WEU-led operation would be US assets dedicated for NATO use. The French, still wary of the true extent of the American commitment to the CJTF concept and to European security in general, and in an attempt to strengthen ESDI, wanted to be able to choose assets for dedication to the WEU before any crisis from a sort of 'buffet line' of hardware and capabilities. The US, however, continued to assert its desire to maintain some management over the use of American assets in WEU-led CJTFs, opposing the proposed French method of allocation.[40] In response to this conflict, the WEU has supplied NATO with a set of illustrative missions which they can envisage themselves undertaking in accordance with the Petersburg Tasks. The list is not exhaustive, but provides an overview of what potential WEU-led operations might require. NATO, in consultation with the WEU, is determining what assets and capabilities would be potentially required for each different scenario.

One further problem that plagued the CJTF concept negotiations was the issue of staffing. The French wanted the CJTF HQs to reflect the European pillar within NATO and the increasing ESDI by appointing more Europeans to senior command positions. The United States responded by giving Europe the post of Deputy Supreme Allied Commander Europe (DSACEUR) as well as agreeing to allocate a number of other positions to the Europeans.

Problems in theory and practice

The CJTF concept, despite its sometimes tortuous negotiation, seems to be, in fact, a stroke of relative genius and answers a number of alliance and national interests. With CJTF, NATO has found a means with which to satisfy urgent political demands (institutional and national), to help bridge the gap between the Alliance's political and military functions, and to enable military planning across the spectrum of operations from 'crisis management to collective defence'.[41] The military utility is apparent, especially with regard to the changed security circumstances in the post-Cold War world and the CJTF ability to meet non-Article 5 situations. The political value is also evident for its effectiveness in justifying the Alliance's continued existence, its encouragement of a stronger European role within the alliance, and its cost-effectiveness in an era of shrinking defence budgets and domestic priorities taking on greater significance in many nations. Approval of the CJTF concept reflects a more European NATO, but also ensures that the United States remains in the central leadership role of the Alliance. The concept still faces many criticisms in practice and in theory, however, and a number of contentious points related to the possibility of a WEU-led CJTF need to be raised.

While the 'separable but not separate' concept is promoted as a tool for the WEU and Europe to find a strengthened role within the alliance, there are doubts about the capability and political will of Europe to lead an operation and act in a crisis situation. There is some question of how well the European allies can accomplish such new missions on their own, with only limited US involvement, and these doubts raise questions about the reality of a WEU-led operation in the future. In this era of shrinking European defence budgets it is less likely that the WEU will have the resources to develop meaningful CJTF capacities. They lack the lift capabilities, do not have the full range of intelligence necessary, and lack the political will and weight of the US. The Europeans have to develop some kind of military clout and some kind of political unity in the European Union to be able to develop their military capacity to levels that impress the rest of the world, and they seem a long way from doing that.

Also compounding the problem of absence of political will is the European emphasis on economic matters within Europe. The attention of the EU has been focused more on achieving Economic and Monetary Union (EMU) than achieving a Common Foreign and Security Policy (CFSP) or further political integration, thus devoting less emphasis to building the capacity of the WEU to sustain ESDI.

During the Cold War, the Europeans came to rely on US guarantees and support of their defence. With the end of the Cold War, Europeans did not shed this outlook and are still hesitant to assert force or undertake operations without the participation and leadership of the United States. The lessons from the peacekeeping operations in Bosnia are a reflection of what can happen from lack of political will on the part of the Europeans as well as the validity that United States participation brings to an operation of this type. NATO was able to succeed in Bosnia where the European Union failed.

Thus, a WEU-led CJTF has the potential to be merely a 'hollow force due to the absence of US combat forces'.[42] The internal civil conflict in Albania also provided an opportunity for collective action on the part of the Europeans, possibly suited to an *ad hoc* CJTF, which they chose not to take and instead left it to the Italians to form a small coalition. One US State Department Official said that 'If the US wants to play on the ground, we have enough leadership power to form a consensus.... Without our leadership, the European institutions often falter.... If we [the United States] wanted to go to Albania as a full operation, we could have...gotten NATO to go along with it and others would go along with it because we took a leadership role.'[43] For the WEU, however, Albania represented a missed opportunity.

The United States and WEU-led CJTFs

The idea of WEU-led CJTFs is obviously appealing from the US perspective for its implications for more equitable contributions and burden-sharing in the alliance. These concerns have been voiced repeatedly in the past. The Clinton Administration has ended the Cold War wariness of the United States and voiced its support for the emerging ESDI. The Administration has also expressed favour for the CJTF concept, adding their desire that these concepts be kept within NATO, and therefore under the watchful eye of the United States. In a speech to the Future Leaders of Europe in Brussels during the 1994 NATO summit, President Clinton reiterated that point in highlighting the sustained US commitment to Europe. He said, 'we ... need to change our security institutions so they can better address ... conflicts and advance Europe's integration. ... But NATO, history's greatest military alliance, must be central to that process.'[44]

The US endorsement for the CJTF concept is not without hesitation or condition, however. As discussed above, many of the assets that could be involved in a CJTF would be US contributions. It makes sense therefore that the United States government will seek to maintain some degree of control over their use. There would not be a US hands-off CJTF operation. With this US desire to maintain some power of authorisation, the reality of support in practice for ESDI development is in question. As explained above, the United States, through the NAC, can veto or rescind an endorsement of an operation that the WEU seeks to undertake. In other words, in the event that the United States opposed a proposed mission, there would be no operation. Not only does this potentially undermine the credibility of the CJTF concept and its implementation, but it also has implications for expectations of US reliability in such situations as well as for the credibility of the WEU, its defence role within the alliance and the reality of ESDI.

The United States finds itself in the contradictory position of wanting to maintain its traditional leadership role in a new NATO while at the same time needing to shed some of the financial and political burdens associated with that role. The CJTF concept will 'benefit the US by enhancing the credibility of the WEU ... and creating greater European responsibility for its own security.'[45] At the same time, however, there is a feeling in the US that this may decrease US influence undesirably in Europe and NATO. Put more simply, the US may not be able to have its cake and eat it too.

Notes

1   Curt Gasteyger in G.A.S.C. Wilson, ed., *British Security 2001* (London: Ministry of Defence, 1996), p. 16.
2   Geoffrey Lee Williams and Alan Lee Williams, *International Terrorism: the Failed Response* (London: Institute for European Defence and Strategic Studies, 1996), p. 47.
3   Paul Kennedy, *Preparing for the Twenty-First Century* (London: HarperCollins, 1993).
4   Paul Eavis and Michael Clarke, *Security after the Cold War: Redirecting Global Resources* (New York: Rowman and Littlefield, 1990).
5   Sean M. Lynn-Jones and Steven Miller, *Global Dangers: Changing Dimensions of International Security* (New York: Basic Books, 1995).
6   Wilson, *British Security 2010*, pp. 179–91.
7   See Lester Thurrow, *The Future of Capitalism* (London: Nicholas Brearly, 1996).
8   See Joseph Joffe, *The Limited Partnership: Europe, the United States and the Burdens of Alliance* (Washington DC: Carnegie Endowment, 1987).
9   I discuss these matters in my forthcoming study, *NATO and the Transatlantic Alliance in the 21st Century* (Macmillan).
10 See Otto Pick, *Collective Security* (London: Charles Knight, 1974).
11 See Javier Solana et al., *NATO Review*, March 1997.
12 See more recent speculation in *The Economist*, 6 December 1997.
13 See Paul Cornish, *Partnership in Crisis: the United States and the Fall and Rise of NATO* (London: Macmillan, 1997).
14 See Geoffrey Lee Williams, *The Logic of Diversity* (London: Institute for European Defence and Strategic Studies, 1992).
15 Ibid.
16 See Alan Lee Williams and Geoffrey Lee Williams, *NATO's Future in the Balance: Time for a Rethink?* (London: Atlantic Council of the United Kingdom, 1995).
17 David Gompert and Stephen Larrabee, *America and Europe: a Partnership for a New Era* (Santa Monica: Rand, 1997).
18 See Douglas Eden, ed., *The Future of the Atlantic Community* (London: Middlesex University Press, 1997), especially Martin Holmes' contribution, pp. 88–102.
19 NATO Press Communiqué M-NAC(DM)-2(96)89, paragraph 4, Brussels, 13 June 1996.
20 Article 5 of the North Atlantic Treaty sets up NATO's traditional collective defence mission.
21 G. Lenzi, 'Introduction', in E. Foster and G. Wilson, eds, *CJTF – a Lifeline for a European Defence Policy?* (London: Royal United Services Institute for Defence Studies, 1997), p. 1.
22 J. Solana, 'NATO's role in Bosnia: charting a new course for the alliance' *NATO Review*, web edition No. 2, March 1996, vol. 44, pp. 3–6.
23 C. Barry, 'NATO's Combined Joint Task Forces in Theory and Practice', *Survival*, vol. 38, no. 1, Spring 1996, p. 84.
24 C. Jean, 'Changing Interstate and Inter-institutional Relations in Europe and NATO', Foster and Wilson, *CJTF*, 1997, p. 40.

25 See the web address: <http://www.nato.int/docu/review/articles/9501–1.htm>.

26 Anthony Cragg, 'Internal Adaptation: Reshaping NATO for the challenges of tomorrow' *NATO Review*, vol. 45, no. 4, July–August 1997, p. 30.

27 M. Bentinck, 'NATO's Structural Reform and the ESDI', in Foster and Wilson, *CJTF*, 1997, p. 80.

28 Cragg, 'Internal Adaptation', p. 34.

29 M. Jackson, 'IFOR and Lessons for Future CJTFs', in Foster and Wilson, *CJTF*, 1997, p. 94.

30 Ibid.

31 Stanley R. Sloan, 'NATO and the United States', in S. Victor Papcosma and Mary Ann Heiss, eds. *NATO in the Post-Cold War Era: Does it Have a Future?* (London: Macmillan, 1995), p. 171.

32 Cragg, 'Internal Adaptation', p. 35.

33 Interview, NATO official, Brussels, 1998 (3).

34 Press Communiqué M-NAC-1(96)63, paragraph 7, Ministerial Meeting of the North Atlantic Council, Berlin, 3 June 1996.

35 See the web adress: <http://www.nato.int/docu/review/articles/9401–2.htm>.

36 NATO official, Brussels, 1998 (1).

37 US Congressional Employee, Washington, DC, 1998 (2), and NATO official.

38 US Congressional Memo on Combined Joint Task Forces, 14 June 1996. Author wishes to remain anonymous.

39 Robert E. Hunter, 'The US and Europe: a parting of the ways or new commitments?' in Foster and Wilson, *CJTF*, p. 75.

40 US Congressional Memo on CJTFs, 14 June 1996.

41 Paul Cornish, 'NATO at the millennium: New missions, new members . . . new strategy?', *NATO Review*, vol. 45, no. 5, September–October 1997, p. 24.

42 US Congressional Memo on CJTFs, 14 June 1996.

43 State Department Official, Washington, DC, 1998.

44 William J. Clinton, *Public Papers of the President of the United States*, Book I, 1 January to 31 July 1994 (Washington, DC: 1995), p. 11.

45 Paul Gebhard, *The US and European Security*, Adelphi Paper 286 (London: 1994), p. 36.

4
The American Policy Debate on NATO Enlargement

William Schneider, Jr

Introduction

In a year precisely seven hundred years prior to my birth (1241), a Mongol archer delivered a well-aimed arrow to the throat of a Polish trumpeter. By doing so, the archer interrupted this trumpeter's sounding of the warning call to residents of Krakow of an impending attack by a column of the army of Batu Khan, grandson of Genghis Kahn. In remembrance of the devastation wrought by the Mongol invasion, the trumpeter's call, the *hejnal mariacki*, has been performed every hour of the day and night from an ancient church in Krakow for the ensuing seven centuries (apart from 1939–45). This remembrance incorporated a brief pause in the cadence commemorating the instant the trumpeter received his mortal wound. This ritual serves as a perpetual reminder to Poles of their enduring vulnerability.[1]

This antiquarian vignette serves as a metaphor for the resilience of the issue of security in public policy in Central and Eastern Europe. The topography of the European Peninsula, its sustained history of migration and tribalism, and the resulting diversity of the region in cultural, political, and economic terms provides the volatile environment that has nurtured armed conflict for millennia. The end of Soviet military power and authority in Europe in 1989, and the collapse of the Soviet state in 1991 have created an opportunity for a new intercontinental approach to security in Europe where an extra-regional player – the United States – needs to assume a central long-term role. Such an arrangement remains *terra incognita* for all, and a source of concern for many. This chapter will explore several aspects of the American debate about European security. This will include both specific American concerns and interests, as well as aspects of the internal European debate that is reflected back into the American policy arena.

American security interests in Europe

An impression held by many, both in Europe and in the US, is that the American military presence in Europe is anomalous, and was narrowly derived from its protracted ideological and military competition with Soviet communism. Proponents of this view argue that the American military presence will (or should) be withdrawn and its security perimeter returned to its nineteenth-century focus on the defence of the Western Hemisphere. While such a point of view exists in some sectors of American political opinion, it is a minority perspective and unlikely to prevail in any debate on the issue of NATO enlargement. The US has been involved in European security for nearly a century. It is widely understood that developments affecting European security eventually affect American interests as well, although the way US interests are engaged is likely to differ in the next decade and US and transatlantic security are intertwined.

US policy has long sought to prevent occupation of the opposite shores of adjacent oceans by hostile powers. This aim has been reflected in the maritime posture implemented by the US Navy throughout its history. This has occurred despite an otherwise inward-focused foreign policy aimed at continental development during the first century of national existence of the US. This posture has matured in the twentieth century as a result of US involvement in global conflict. Twentieth-century experience has produced a diplomatic focus on the development of alliance networks in both Europe and East Asia. The aim of these alliances has been to secure US access in times of military confrontation, and to assure a 'seat at the table' in economic and political aspects of regional affairs. Europe's political diversity and the limited battle-space of the European Plain make coalition warfare a desirable approach from the US perspective. This has been best implemented through a multilateral alliance.

In Asia, where vast distances in political, cultural and military terms preclude a regional alliance, the US government has sought to secure its aims in the region through a network of bilateral military alliances. These bilateral alliances have been supplemented by a mix of bilateral access, pre-positioning, training, and other security-related protocols. A post-Second World War broadening of US interests took place in the Middle East in both the Levant (due to US sponsorship of the establishment of the State of Israel) and the Persian Gulf. The latter arrangements have evolved from informal understandings of support to more formalised arrangements in the form of Defence Co-operation Agreements (DCA), especially since the Gulf War (1991).

It is in Europe that American interests are most well-established and supported by a broad political consensus. A secure and free Europe is a crucial factor in domestic economic prosperity, since Europe is America's largest trading partner. The international trade sector has grown from 5 per cent of the US economy in the 1960s to 25 per cent today. The importance of international political stability in creating an environment able to sustain American economic dynamism is a new feature of American foreign policy which responds to the enriched character of American interests abroad in the late twentieth century.

The end of a common external threat from the former Soviet Union has produced a new situation which jeopardises American interests – to the possible exclusion of the US from Europe. The American response to these new circumstances contributes to an understanding of American post-Cold War diplomacy. The US has opposed the emergence of a single strong power in Europe as the Soviet threat ended. Hence, the vigorous American support for German unification following the opening of the Berlin Wall in 1989, American advocacy of the cause of NATO and EU enlargement, achieving a broad definition of Europe to include Turkey and the former Soviet states west of the Ural Mountains, and insistence on the post-Cold War primacy of transatlantic rather than Eurocentric institutions. This approach contrasts sharply with the views of some European states. Indeed, some US officials have seen European efforts to revive (e.g. WEU) or create *de novo* (e.g. European Corps) European institutions, especially those with security-related functions that exclude the US, as an effort to separate the US from involvement in European affairs. The proposition that the EU be given a security role is likely to be seen as a negative development that will undermine the ability of NATO to act in a security crisis in Europe.

Europe's history of local or regional conflicts metastasising into confrontations which have directly engaged American interests, has stimulated a political as well as a military requirement for a permanent American military presence in Europe, despite the end of the Soviet threat. An American military presence makes the United States a diplomatic party to conflict in Europe as it evolves, rather than waiting for a crisis to mature to trigger US engagement. Its parallel leadership of NATO – the only security institution in Europe with the infrastructure to act and sustain multinational military operations – serves American interests as well. NATO is seen by US policy-makers as an instrument to facilitate the management of intra-European rivalries that might otherwise mature in a manner hostile to US interests.

The Gulf War has intensified the view of US authorities of the importance of the US military presence in Europe. The US presence in Europe can facilitate a response to 'out-of-area' contingencies, including the Levant, the Gulf and Africa. In particular, the US European presence facilitates support for the policy aim of denying control by a hostile power over Gulf-region energy production. Hence, American tenacity in resisting a French appeal to assume the military leadership of NATO's Southern Region. The US 6th Fleet deployed in the Mediterranean Sea has often been over-equipped for the NATO mission to provide the 'excess capacity' needed to support extra-regional contingencies, either unilaterally or multilaterally as required. Missions as diverse as Operation Desert Storm and civilian evacuations from sundry African conflicts have been supported by the US European presence. Its utility in implementing American policy aims to secure a measure of political stability in parts of the world within convenient reach of Europe makes it likely that a military presence will be a long-term characteristic of American policy aims in Europe.

The unsettled political contours of the evolution of the former Soviet Union are an added motivation for the US to remain a major player in Europe. The US seeks to prevent the re-emergence either of the former Soviet Union or the Russian Empire. Preserving the independence of the constituent states of the former Soviet Union, especially those West of the Ural Mountains, constitutes an important dimension of this policy. This in turn requires some means of incorporating the European states of the former Soviet Union into a European security system, though the immediate aim is less to protect them from an extra-European threat than from other European states.

Post-Cold War military modernisation in the United States

The US response to the absence of a coherent single adversary or adversary coalition diverges significantly from the approach taken by several of the major European nations. This divergence could have a longer-term political effect. The likely path of American military modernisation has been apparent for several years, but was crystallised in the Quadrennial Defence Review (QDR) published by the Department of Defence in mid-May 1997. The QDR ratified the aim to recapitalise the US armed forces through the incorporation of information-driven technologies derived largely from rapid civil-sector advances in computation, signal processing, telecommunications, software engineering, and microelectronics during the investment boom in the 1980s.[2]

The US inventory of analog-based equipment is being rendered obsolescent at a rapid rate. The reason for this is that, unless suitably modified, analog equipment cannot receive and process targeting and related time-sensitive information generated by a rapidly increasing network of sensors based in space, unmanned air vehicles (UAVs), manned aircraft, surface naval combatants, submarines and ground-based systems. Analog systems will remain dependent on a sluggish analog military communications system that will always prevent a near-real time response to the emergence of military targets. The 'fog of war' will remain an important obstacle to political–military effectiveness but is unlikely to be a decisive factor with advanced conventional warfare technologies. Further, military establishments which fail to recapitalise will be condemned to maintain relatively large force structures to sustain military effectiveness; a difficult task in the fiscally austere post-Cold War environment.

In the digital domain, information generated by this array of sensors, processing, and precision weapon systems makes it possible for both military commanders and their political leadership to share simultaneously a near-real time awareness of a rapidly evolving military or political situation. Complementary platforms and weapon systems able to exploit information in a digital format will be able to achieve major performance gradients, thus enabling the current military effectiveness of the existing force to be achieved with far smaller military forces. While the substitution of capital for labour in military institutions has been the trend throughout the industrial era, the transition to information-driven technologies is producing quantum changes in the relationship between resource inputs and military effectiveness.

A recent US military exercise conducted two months prior to the completion of the QDR illustrated the opportunities emerging from the absorption of information technologies by the armed forces. The US Army's Advanced Warfare Experiment (Force XXI) was conducted in a California desert training centre (Fort Irwin) over a two-week period involving hundreds of combat vehicles modified to employ digital systems to process information provided by space, airborne and ground-based sensors. These data were linked to appropriate weapon systems able to exploit the information and accurately engage targets at a considerable distance from the point of launch. The implications for military operations were significant, and perhaps fundamental. While the long-run implications of these developments for American alliances are favourable, short- and medium-term concerns arise.

The exercise revealed that performance improvements were substantial as a result of the ability of military units at all levels to exploit digital information to engage targets promptly. The performance of these specially equipped units against forces lacking an information-dominated infrastructure was very high, permitting significant reductions in the number of combatant platforms in a given military unit to sustain unit effectiveness.

The QDR recommended that the DoD propagate the transformation of the armed forces from its industrial/analog configuration to an information-based digital structure. The Clinton Administration has agreed to do so. While full implementation is likely to consume a decade or more at current resource levels, partial implementation has been underway for several years and was reflected in some recent US military campaigns, including Operation Desert Storm in Iraq in 1991 and Bosnia since 1995. These developments have some near- and medium-term implications for US alliance structures, particularly in Europe.

Allies as burdens?

The impact of advances in military technology derived from information-related developments on military performance has had the effect of exacerbating the gap between the capabilities of US forces and most of their allies, especially in Europe. Throughout the Cold War period, the 'division of labour' between the nations of the alliance drove asymmetries between allied nations and the United States. This was especially the case in the ability of the US to mount and sustain expeditionary operations, theatre-wide manoeuvre, deep-strike operations, and intelligence-collection and -processing. The implications of the extent of US modernisation recommended by the QDR will extend this asymmetry throughout the spectrum of military operations from close combat to deep strike operations.

This in turn has produced a new form of the Cold War era 'burden sharing' argument. The Cold War diplomatic and political tensions between the US and its European allies revolved around 'inputs' – especially the growth rate of aggregate defence expenditure. The incipient post-Cold War intra-alliance debate is about 'outputs' in the form of military performance, especially in performance metrics needed to facilitate intra-alliance military operations. *In extremis*, the divergence in US and allied capabilities, if sustained, will significantly limit the ability of the forces to interoperate in coalition warfare.

Of more immediate concern is the inability of Europe to engage military modernisation issues as a result of its preoccupation with the need to restructure its economy to meet the demands of the economics of the twenty-first century. Restructuring may be a protracted process as a result of Europe's political realignment as reflected in the most recent UK, French and German national elections. The issue has nevertheless been raised in the United States: to what extent will allies be able to perform effectively in military operations sponsored or sanctioned by NATO? It is in any event a dimension of the US political debate concerning NATO expansion. Allied military modernisation is subject to Congressional and news-media scrutiny.

Improving alliance effectiveness

The effectiveness of NATO as an alliance in both political and military terms depends upon its ability to act. The Cold War environment produced a number of important capabilities enabling the alliance to act effectively and that serve as an enduring legacy of the alliance to European security. The most important elements are NATO's logistics infrastructure, its command–control–communication (C3) system, and its integrated air defence system embedded in its network of ground- and air-based (Airborne Warning and Control System – AWACS) radars and command centres as well as area and terminal air defences. These are necessary, but not sufficient to assure NATO's ability to act in the future. Two key alliance capabilities are needed: situation awareness and theatre missile defence.

Situation awareness: Alliance decisions require consensus among its membership, an issue that will be more difficult to achieve with present alliance surveillance assets when NATO membership is enlarged. A common appreciation of the situation producing an evolving crisis is indispensable to common political and military action. This is now in being to cope with airborne threats to the alliance as a result of earlier investment in NATO's air defence network. This capability was an important factor in the ability of the alliance to extend its 'reach' into the Balkans in the management of this protracted crisis. The future capability needed to provide a basis for common action in NATO is alliance ground surveillance (AGS). The US candidate for this mission, its Joint Surveillance and Targeting System (JSTARS) was employed in its R&D configuration in Operation Desert Storm in 1991, and in a production configuration in support of the NATO deployment to the Balkans in 1995–96. The JSTARS capability, the product of a $3 billion US investment, is designed to provide theatre-wide near real-time situation awareness of activity on the ground. It was employed in the Advanced Warfare Experiment (Force XXI) exercise previously discussed. Without NATO AGS, the 'fog of war' is likely to serve as a barrier to common action by the alliance due to the difficulty of obtaining such a timely appreciation of the circumstances in an intense crisis through traditional diplomatic and intelligence capabilities. The QDR has ratified a production decision for JSTARS. Both France and the UK are working on national systems for the AGS mission, though neither has a system that will provide theatre-wide support to NATO operations.

Theatre missile defence (TMD): An important international military development that emerged in the 1980s, and is likely to mature in the early years of the twenty-first century is a common military (cruise, guided, and ballistic) missile threat to Europe from states outside Europe. The Cold War proved to be (inadvertently) constructive in constraining the international diffusion of missile technology. The centrifugal forces unleashed in the former Soviet empire as it collapsed, however, have produced new regional and sub-regional incentives for the acquisition of missiles to meet local security needs. Sophisticated manufacturing technology from the civil sector is serving to lower the cost of military missile production (as well as that of weapons of mass destruction, the cost of nuclear weapon development and production has declined exponentially since 1945), making it accessible to most developing nations in Eurasia and North Africa. North Korea has developed long-range missiles for customers able to put Europe at risk of nuclear or biological weapons attack. The 1300–km range North Korean No Dong missile has been sold to and tested by Iran as its Shahab 3 missile (in July 1998). North Korea successfully tested its 6000-km range Tepo-dong missile in August 1998. Were this in the hands of Iran or Libya, all of Europe could be at risk of missile attack. NATO needs a common basis for defence against missile attack – the weapon of choice for a wide range of military operations. A number of land-, sea-, air- and space-based TMD alternatives have emerged from US, European, and Israeli research on the subject. Israel appears likely to be the first nation to deploy a nation-wide TMD system (Arrow), with Japan likely to follow in the early years of the twenty-first century. The new missile currently under development by Iran will bring Europe within range of land-based missiles launched from the region, and others will follow. The absence of a common capability to deter or defend against missile attack is likely to diminish the effectiveness of NATO as a military organisation.

Policy issues in NATO enlargement

The enlargement of NATO and its consequences is important as a policy issue in its own terms. The debate extends beyond the ratification of the enlargement of NATO as such: the post-ratification debate may also serve as a proxy in the US debate for the nature, scope, and degree of US involvement in European security affairs in the first quarter of the twenty-first century.[3] The debate is likely to engage a wide variety of US interests ranging from military security to trade to cultural issues. The security imperative of the Cold War period that permitted security issues to be addressed on their own merits, separately from other bilateral and multilateral issues, no longer obtains. Long-term security considerations for the United States are likely to be embedded in a larger and more colourful mosaic of international considerations. The move of the EU into the security arena will intensify discussions about the US role in Europe and NATO's relationship to that role.

The American post-ratification debate will emerge around the issues associated with authorising the enlargement of NATO membership within the Treaty to which the United States is a party, and subsequently the financing of the US share of the costs associated with the infrastructure of NATO enlargement. As this will involve Congressional consent, the debate is likely to be highly political, but as has been the case with recent US trade liberalisation debates, neither partisan nor intensely ideological.

There have been some precursors to this sort of debate: the most significant parallel was the protracted controversy over the Mansfield amendment first offered in 1968. This amendment proposed to limit and eventually reduce the US military presence in Europe. The issue was less about cost than political aims and American international involvement. To this extent, the debate over the Mansfield amendment through the mid-1970s served as a proxy for the manner in which the US would confront Soviet military power in Europe for the balance of the Cold War. The effective response of the US Administration's leadership and its Congressional allies contributed to the stabilisation and strengthening of the US commitment in Europe. This in turn made the 1983 decision on GLCM/Pershing theatre missile deployments to offset Soviet SS-20 and SS-23 deployments in Europe possible. This decision contributed to the subsequent weakening of the Soviet political and military system in Europe.

Because the debate on NATO's future is likely to be a proxy for more fundamental issues of long-term US security policy, a number of concerns are likely to be important elements of the debate. Among them are likely to be the following:

1. Military issues

The ability of an enlarged security alliance to perform effectively and undertake timely decisions will be an important feature of the debate. This broad question can be divided into a number of subordinate elements.

- *Allied military capabilities*: The ability of the allies to field effective military capabilities will emerge as an issue, both from a resource ('input') and performance ('output') perspective. The all-but-inevitable abandonment of conscription in continental Europe will force Europe to face the true cost of military manpower, and is likely to affect resource allocation that could slow the rate of modernisation (shift from labour to capital-intensive military systems) in Europe. Europe is currently seeking to recapitalise its combat aircraft, theatre airlift, main battle tank, and frigate inventories. Europe's ability to generate appropriate military capabilities over the course of the next decade will be discussed.
- *The readiness of new accessions to NATO to assume the burden(s) of NATO membership will be a significant policy issue.* The decline of public support for NATO membership in Central Europe (apart from Poland), and the reluctance of governments in that area to allocate resources to finance the costs of achieving interoperability could emerge as a significant issue in Congressional debates as the cost to the US to facilitate interoperability becomes apparent.
- *Support for peacekeeping and other NATO-sanctioned out-of-area operations*: The ability of the alliance to accept post-Cold War missions will be an important dimension of the Congressional and public perception of the post-Cold War benefit of the NATO alliance and the value of its enlargement. An expansion of the scope of NATO operations from repelling an armed attack to its employment in the Balkans is an encouraging development, but NATO resolve elsewhere remains to be tested. The reluctance or division among the NATO members concerning enforcement of UN resolutions in Iraq has increased bilateralism (in this case, US–UK) outside of the alliance structure.

2. Political issues

While NATO is a military alliance, the political terms within which the alliance operates are a central feature of the debate. The underlying issue is the post-Cold War architecture of the European security system – not merely the issue of adding three (or eventually five or more) new members. The absence of any modern experience in dealing with Central and East European states as independent entities has caused a renewed interest in ancient national, ethnic, cultural, economic, political and tribal rivalries which may encumber rather than enhance the political cohesion of the alliance.

- *The role of Russia in NATO decision-making*: Congressional attitudes toward Russia remain equivocal despite the collapse of Soviet military power and Russia's lively political pluralism. The underlying theme of imperialistic nationalism in elements of Russia's opposition, and the fitful movement of Russia toward democratic institutions and market capitalism gives pause to those who hoped successful reform would have emerged from the $50+ billion invested by the international community in bilateral and multilateral aid projects in Russia since 1991. The pretentious but ambiguous 'Founding Act on Mutual Relations, Co-operation, and Security Between NATO and the Russian Federation' signed in May 1998 has already provoked controversy. Russia proclaims it will have a veto over NATO actions through the newly created NATO Permanent Joint Council, and asserts that NATO has agreed to far-reaching restrictions. President Yeltsin asserted, 'Nuclear weapons are not to be deployed, no storage facilities are to be used, the infrastructure abandoned by the Warsaw pact is not to be used for this. This is exceptionally important.'[4] The White House has fudged a response to determined diplomatic and Congressional inquiries. The diminishing coherence of the Russian state subsequent to the devaluation of the ruble on 17 August 1998 has made the future of Russia in Europe even more ambiguous and worrisome.
- *Resolution of residual conflict(s) between new members*: The fact that many of the Central and East European states were created through arbitrary boundaries subsequent to the First World War is widely understood. Underlying tensions that have been submerged in totalitarian domination for more than half a century could break out in ways difficult for the US government to predict, that could draw the US into Europe's unplumbed trove of internecine conflict. Romania and Hungary have been energetically pursuing diplomatic efforts to resolve the best-known of these disputes, but many more remain to be addressed, and uncounted others remain to be discovered.
- *NATO political decision-making*: Apart from the question of integrating the NATO–Russian agreement into its decision-making, the implica-

tions of an increasing membership pose a risk to decisive action, and hence, to Congressional support. The Greek–Turkish dispute has already affected NATO and EU decision-making adversely; enlargement increases these risks.

- *Financing NATO enlargement*: Measuring political commitment through financial inputs holds endless potential for discord. Europe's stressful fiscal circumstances and opposition to the enlargement of any European institutions (including NATO) is likely to cause them to receive US Congressional appeals for financial 'burden sharing' with little enthusiasm. A reluctance of the existing NATO membership to finance the infrastructure and related common costs of enlargement will compound Congressional *angst* about what will almost certainly be a slow pace of modernisation among the prospective new members.
- *NATO endgame expectations*: US government leadership rhetoric has been scarce on where NATO enlargement is heading. While this is generally seen as enlarging a successful security system for Europe, others are urgently seeking membership, including those whose membership would increase tensions with Russia. Romania and Slovenia are conducting energetic and effective public relations campaigns in Washington in support of their interest in NATO membership, and in some ways are better qualified in military terms than Hungary and the Czech Republic. The Baltic States and Ukraine are also potential candidates for membership. NATO membership is seen as crucial to the process of economic transformation as an instrument to reduce economic 'transaction costs' – an implicit premium paid by nations deemed as insecure sites for investment and business operations by commercial and financial markets. Miscues in the management of the long-term vision for the European security system could undermine the prospects for public support. The impact on NATO of a parallel EU-based European security system is a concern to the US in discerning the direction of European security.
- *Costs to the US of NATO enlargement*: Under the Clinton Administration's 1995 Warsaw Initiative, the US Government has been providing $100 million in bilateral military aid to the former states of the Warsaw Pact, but primarily to the three economically successful Visegrad states – Poland, Hungary and the Czech Republic. The infrastructure costs financed through NATO will be significantly larger. The slow pace of European defence modernisation to an information-based force is an alliance problem. The new Central European members have yet to make a transition from their inventory of Soviet-era equipment. There have been some recent indications that they may

procure older Western systems, but little change has materialised to date. As a result, the cost to the US of providing the supplemental modern C3I and transport infrastructure to NATO is high. The annual cost of Balkan operations to the United States is approximately $3 billion.

The emergence of the post-ratification NATO post-enlargement debate in the US is likely to occur when the US and Europe are at different stages of the business cycle. This will undoubtedly affect the political tone of the debate, with some on the US side insisting on greater effort on the part of Europe than it is prepared to offer. In addition, the realignment of European politics from leadership by conservative parties to control by some mutation of the formerly militant socialist parties in Western Europe and a restoration of bureaucratic communist rule in parts of Central Europe may pose further challenges to transatlantic cooperation. President Yeltsin is seen by many in the Congress as a flawed and transitional leadership figure who is unlikely to be the final arbiter of the form in which the Russian state ultimately emerges from three-quarters of a century of Communist rule.

The US government and the Congress have ultimately supported NATO enlargement, but further developments outside NATO that confront US interests could undermine US political resolve in Europe. The southward expansion of Russia through a loosening of the barriers created by the Conventional Forces in Europe (CFE) Treaty could jeopardise other US interests in the Caucasus region and the Middle East. US Government acquiescence in Russia's demands to modify the CFE Treaty to sustain its deployments in Chechnya created an added dimension to the NATO enlargement issue.[5] A revived Iraqi challenge to the outcome of the 1991 Gulf War has produced diminished rather than enhanced alliance security cooperation. These cases illustrate rather than exhaust the range of issues which could intervene in the protracted American policy debate about the US security role in Europe.

Notes

1 Norman Davies, *A History of Europe* (New York: Oxford University Press, 1996), p. 365.
2 William Cohen, Secretary of Defence, *Quadrennial Defence Commission Final Report* (Washington, DC: Office of the Secretary of Defence, 15 May 1997).

3 For a detailed discussion of US Government views on NATO enlargement, see the *Report to the Congress on the Enlargement of the North Atlantic Treaty Organisation: Rationale, Benefits, Costs, and Implications* (Washington, DC: US Department of State, Bureau of European and Canadian Affairs, 24 February 1997). These views were amplified in testimony by the Secretary of State (Madeleine K. Albright) before the Committee on Armed Services of the US Senate, 23 April 1997.

4 Quoted in 'The New NATO: "powerful force" or "total gridlock"?', *Russian Reform Monitor* (Washington, DC, 20 May 1997).

5 An illustration of opposing arguments to the US government's approach to NATO enlargement and its dealings with the Russian leadership is contained in 'Making Moscow Happy', *Wall Street Journal*, 16 May 1997.

5
The Strategic Environment: the Next Twenty Years' Crisis?

Alan Lee Williams

The strategic environment remains the most crucial and salient factor affecting the decision to acquire weapons of mass destruction (WMD) by nation-states living in a state of nature despite the hopeful atmosphere generated by the end of the Cold War. The strategic environment is difficult to predict but it appears to be becoming more volatile.

We can expect the next decade or so to be chaotic and turbulent. The strategic American power will remain dominant but also diminished by neo-isolationism, while Europe is assailed by nationalism along its rimlands and the spectre of mass migrations. The process of European integration will slow down in the short term in the face of intractable problems associated with the merger of governmental systems, the merger of political systems, the merger of economic systems, the merger of peoples and societies and removal of state boundaries.

The increase in the size of the European Union from 15 to 20+ nations by the year 2020 or beyond will mark the emergence of a wider and essentially non-federal Europe with an inner core of 'federated' states with a single currency and a common macro-economic policy. 'The enlargement of NATO will complement the enlargement of the EU, a parallel process which also for its part contributes significantly to extending security to the new democracies in the East.'[1]

The Alliance took a momentous step towards building an undivided Europe when Foreign Ministers signed documents in December 1997 paving the way for NATO's opening to three new members. However, NATO's future relevance depends on its seriously going 'out of area' if it wants to avoid going into irreversible decline. NATO is adept at flexibility and could transform itself into an 'agent of change' that could effectively address contemporary security issues in their broader definition. The enlargement of NATO by only three or four countries will be easier to handle. But it also carries the risk of creating a new dividing line in Europe, with NATO members on one hand and non-members on the other. In Europe there is a real danger of fragmentation in both NATO and the EU unless and until the issues of 'widening' and 'deepening' are resolved through sweeping institutional change and redefinition of purpose.

It is likely that Japan and China will emerge over the next 10 to 15 years as military hegemons to match their economic dominance of Asia, while the population explosion in Africa and Asia will precipitate new global dangers. Both Europe and America will face a multiplicity of missile threats of differing ranges and warheads over the two decades. These missile systems will be in the hands of developing countries reflecting the new axis of global conflict, the North–South conflict, replacing the past East–West divide. The manifest dangers arising from radical nationalism, ethnic strife and religious fundamentalism will affect Europe as well as other parts of the globe.

The Yugoslav civil war is but an awful warning of what is yet to come in the Commonwealth of Independent States (CIS) and more especially within the Russian Federation. The Balkans will continue to bubble and boil, threatening a wider conflict if NATO peacekeeping forces are removed. Ethnic cleansing and humanitarian catastrophe in Eastern Europe will again shock world opinion and threaten the stability of NATO's neighbours.

A possible way to avoid a crisis in the region is through NATO's Partnership for Peace (PfP) programme and Contact Groups, whereby non-NATO countries are involved in joint exercises or consultation. The PfP countries very much want to join NATO, but will not be invited in the near future for one reason or another. In the last few years, however, NATO has established close working relationships of cooperation and partnership with nearly every country in the Euro-Atlantic region. The Euro-Atlantic Partnership Council (EAPC) builds on the successful experience with the North Atlantic Co-operation Council (NACC) and PfP. It provides a forum to oversee and develop all NATO activities with partner countries, including an enhanced PfP, and is designed as a framework to strengthen relations of all Partners not only with NATO but also among themselves. In EAPC, allies and partners are exploring possibilities for regional security cooperation. By the enhancement, PfP will be even better capable of creating a pattern of interaction, cooperation and joint activities among the military and defence structures of the allies and 27 partner countries and contribute in a very practical way to NATO's goal of building cooperative security in Europe. Cooperation over the K-For policing of Kosovo is an important talisman.

With respect to arms control, the reduction in the nuclear stockpiles of the US and Russia under the Strategic Arms Limitation Treaties (START I and II) will be adhered to with increasing difficulty. These agreements will be subject to agreed breakouts, rather like the elastic interpretation attached to the implementation of the reductions of conventional armed forces in Europe (CFE) by the former Soviet Union. US–Russian relations are likely to be under considerable stress and strain, with NATO–Europe still denying membership to Russia but moving towards integrating the countries of Central and Eastern Europe (CEE) into its structures. This might well precipitate a twenty-year crisis. The enlargement, said Robert Hunter, the former US Ambassador to NATO, must not undercut the strength of democracy in Russia. It is necessary to appreciate the Russian sensitivities regarding the extension of NATO to its borders. NATO should be given a sphere of competence including CEE, yet be willing to provide Russia with reassurance about its right to maintain an acceptable *status quo* within the CIS.

A new initiative by NATO to introduce a special security forum to reassure Russia about enlargement was announced in early February 1997. This is the creation of a NATO–Russian Council. It is important for security and stability in the whole of Europe that the USA and Western Europe remain on good terms with the Russian Federation. NATO stood just as firmly by its conviction that Russia could became a valuable strategic partner in helping to build a stable Europe. The result was the Founding Act on Mutual Relations, Co-operation and Security between NATO and Russia, signed in Paris in May 1997. Through the NATO–Russia Permanent Joint Council (PJC), it gives Russia a voice not a veto on alliance activities. NATO has made a bold step in bringing Russia closer to the Euro-Atlantic structures.

The European Union (EU) will be moving towards a heightened defence identity through the WEU–NATO nexus but with the conduct of security policies still firmly in the hands of national governments acting through a Europeanised NATO. Europe's chief weakness will be its ongoing failure to invest enough in communications, command, control and intelligence facilities (C3i), as well as its collective failure to increase expenditure on research and development (R&D).

Difficulties will arise within the EU over the establishment of a common foreign and security policy (CFSP) as peacekeeping and possible peace-enforcement policies are exacerbated by national differences. Germany will experience the most difficulty in adjusting to its newfound peacekeeping responsibilities in which both Britain and France will be conditionally committed.

NATO could split over the issue of power projection and the question of global reach. The next decade will most probably see heightened conflict in the Southern Hemisphere, leading to attempted mass migration to the North. This will be strongly resisted by the European Union, still coping with indigenous racism in France, Germany and Britain. The consequent drift of refugees, possibly as many as 30 million, is likely therefore to exacerbate national and ethnic conflicts within Europe and along its rimlands. Nationalities and inner cities could explode into violence; thus, international terrorism is likely to increase against the developed world. The most likely insurgent groups will be those driven by Islamic fundamentalists or religious radicals opposed to Western postmodern secular society. The dangers involved in the spread of Weapons of Mass Destruction (WMD) must therefore be seen against the backdrop of this strategic environment.

The growing tendency to acquire WMD and ballistic missiles appears to reflect a number of complex and contradictory motivations which nation-states confront when deciding to promote their national interests. Two well-established motivations appear to predominate: military or strategic ambitions and meta-strategic power play. The former depends upon perceived threats to specific national interests or goals and the latter is derived in part from the prestige which nuclear weapons in particular have historically bestowed upon their possessors.

Between 1941 and 1990 an analysis of seven nuclear nations, which included the United States, USSR, Britain, France, China, India and Israel, identified some of the considerations that led to their decisions to go nuclear. These included world-power status, national security, ideological and local area leadership and alliance obligations.

Similar, if not identical, postures are likely to be adopted by new nuclear powers, although there could be less reassuring crazy nuclear actors as well. Historically, the nuclear postures ranged widely from deterrence by matching an adversary's arsenal, or deterrence by denial of victory (the superpowers), deterrence based on second centre and insurance policy (the UK), proportional deterrence and insurance policy (France), people's war with minimum deterrent (China), insurance against future need (India and Pakistan) and deterrence by denial of victory (Israel). Is it to be expected that future nuclear weapons states will replicate similar postures? Might Pakistan, for example, develop a first-use strategy?

Given the assumption that nuclear weapons and other weapons of mass destruction will spread to more nations over the next 20 years or so, what risks are likely to arise with respect to NATO–Europe and its closest allies? Put simply: the risk of nuclear blackmail by Third World nuclear powers, or the risks of nuclear fallout from a nuclear attack or exchange among such powers affecting NATO and its associated PfP and Combined Joint Task Force (CJTF) states.

More crucially perhaps, there is the risk of weapons-grade material falling into the hands of non-state actors, which cannot be entirely ruled out and as a result of which terrorist-type demands could be made against legitimate political entities. This could threaten lives and property on an unacceptable scale. Thus, NATO is right to regard the pursuit of a non-proliferation policy as a top alliance priority through participation in or support for arms control arrangements (e.g. Non-Proliferation, Comprehensive Test Ban and Anti-Ballistic Missile treaties). Yet, alliance support for arms control must not obscure its limitations whether it is pursued bilaterally, multilaterally or indeed unilaterally within a formal or informal framework.

The traditional objectives of arms control, of course, have been to enhance global and regional stability, to reduce the likelihood of war and to reduce the consequences and costs of war if it occurs. These objectives must continue to be pursued and there are a number of leading questions which must be answered:

- What are the real prospects for full implementation of the revamped CFE and START agreements given the volatile internal situation in Russia today?
- Should arms control remain a major focus of NATO's interest and energy in the decades ahead?
- In what ways can arms control be used to diminish the threats to regional and international security?
- Should the US and Russia attempt to move beyond the START process?

Further questions revolve around restraints on nuclear modernisation, the notion of operational arms control and counter-strategic capabilities. We need to assess the threats posed by the proliferation of conventional and unconventional weapons, and whether nuclear weapons do constitute the greatest threat. How effective have the Nuclear Proliferation Treaty (NPT) and Missile Technology Control Regime (MTCR) been? Should the Anti-Ballistic Missile (ABM) Treaty be renegotiated and, finally, what new non-proliferation initiatives should be pursued?

The questions are endless: the answers few.

More pressing questions arise, of course, over more immediate issues with regard to both vertical and horizontal nuclear proliferation. Clearly, vertical proliferation as measured by the number of nuclear tests conducted and the size of the nuclear stockpiles held by the permanent members of the UN Security Council have been or appear to be much less threatening to world peace than horizontal proliferation among unstable authoritarian 'pariah' or 'rogue' states. Such states, like North Korea, Iraq or Iran, the classic examples, may wish to acquire the means of physical intimidation and of mass destruction in order to wage aggressive war. More probably, their object is to attempt the psychological browbeating of local rivals in a protracted stand-off, or to deter a great power from intervening in favour of the *status quo* to 'correct' their disruptive behaviour.

The acquisition of nuclear weaponry together with the development of sophisticated means of delivery of weapons in excess of 600 miles by so-called 'pariah' states will become a major destabilising factor in the twenty-first century if the number of nuclear powers continues to multiply. It already has. Remember that Iraq, Iran and North Korea have all displayed a strong and unremitting nuclear ambition. The emergence of such nuclear powers, whose political elites have powerful incentives to appear to behave ruthlessly, or indeed even irrationally, for domestic reasons, are only likely to be checked by similarly armed states, if at all. The dangers therefore speak for themselves and are rising. Arms control ring-fencing is in danger of breaking down in the face of this challenge.

The existence of a number of nuclear-capable powers, apart from the five official members of the 'nuclear club' (the permanent members of the United Nations Security Council), has revealed the very limited effectiveness of arms control measures. Thus Israel, Pakistan and India have already acquired nuclear weapons, while South Africa claims to have had but abandoned them and North Korea, Libya, Iraq,[2] Algeria and possibly others, notably Iran, are all engaged in nuclear weapons programmes. The trend is ominous.

Iraq's pretensions to become a nuclear-capable power, for example, have already twice provoked an external response: first from Israel, and then from the US-led coalition enforcing UN Security Council resolutions during and following the Gulf War. The work of the United Nations Special Commission (UNSCOM) in Iraq is likely to remain incomplete.

North Korea in 1994 also provoked an American response. Yet, after a tense stand-off with South Korea and the United States, a nuclear pact between America and North Korea was agreed. Under this pact, North Korea was required to abandon its nuclear weapons programme in return for improved economic and diplomatic relations and two reactors worth

$4 billion (£2.6 billion) which do not produce weapon-grade plutonium. (By 1998 there was some doubt about the viability of this deal.)

Thus, two models of arms control outside the formal diplomatic framework associated with formal negotiations have emerged: the stick and the carrot, so to speak. Could this be the model for the twenty-first century?

Both approaches are equally valid and should be supported; but their limitations should be recognised and made more explicit. The spread of long-range missiles and the proliferation of precision-guided weaponry, together with the dissemination of chemical and biological WMDs, will necessitate more than the carrot-and-stick approach.

It is clear that a much more coherent approach is needed to deal with the spread of high-tech strategic weaponry. This may well require very different thinking that repudiates the idea of a kind of moral symmetry once nations have acquired nuclear weapons. It will be necessary, if this logic is accepted, to dispute or reject the current interpretation attached to Article 6 of the Non-Proliferation Treaty (NPT) which seeks to link vertical proliferation to horizontal proliferation. There is, for example, little evidence to justify the belief that a diminution in the number of warheads possessed by permanent members of the Security Council necessarily diminishes the pursuit of nuclear status by smaller powers. In any event, whether this argument is accepted or not by Third World governments, the causal connection between vertical and horizontal proliferation has been weakened by START I and II as far as the US and Russia are concerned. Therefore, vertical proliferation is not the problem: horizontal proliferation of WMD will be the scourge of the next century, the coming crisis of the next 20 years.

The evidence appears to suggest that prospective nuclear powers have their own compelling strategic reasons for acquiring nuclear weapons other than those allegedly arising from the vertical proliferation of nuclear warheads. The logic of Article 6 of the NPT has been greatly weakened by the change in strategic realities following the collapse of the Soviet Union and of the Cold War.

The rejection of the logic of Article 6 rests on the distinction between the existence of 'responsible' nuclear powers and more or less 'irresponsible' powers. This argument should not rest on the assumption that all future proliferators are irresponsible: indeed a strong case can be made for allowing a controlled expansion of the number of nuclear powers. In any event, it might prove inevitable. It is probably not yet possible, if at all, to be certain about the criteria for establishing the distinction between responsible and irresponsible powers because it would be invidious to identify certain countries which should be considered 'irresponsible' beyond the obvious few: e.g. North Korea, Iran, Iraq and Libya, and *not* Israel, India or Pakistan.

Yet, once it has been agreed to which presumed category a country belongs, the so-called carrot-and-stick procedures should be adopted to deal with countries committing a flagrant violation of the NPT, constituting an illegal breakout as defined by the International Atomic Energy Authority (IAEA). NATO's Strategic Concept, endorsed at the Washington summit in April 1999, recognises the need for a policy aimed at opposing the unbridled proliferation of nuclear, biological and chemical weapons and their means of delivery, such as ballistic and Cruise missiles. Proliferation could constitute a direct threat to the NATO security area, particularly in the Gulf region. The development of NATO's new function outside the treaty area was therefore closely related to this development. Some countries, such as Iraq and North Korea, did not abide by international treaty obligations. Other countries were acquiring weapons of mass destruction and delivery systems which could constitute a direct threat to NATO countries. These developments could increase instability in potential crisis areas. This could cause risks for NATO since proliferation has been taking place in North Africa, the Middle East and South-West Asia, all adjacent to the NATO area. There was therefore an immediate need to develop a policy to deal with proliferation.

NATO should be able to fashion a *comprehensive counter-proliferation strategy* which goes beyond adherence to a negative and often platitudinous arms control policy. The matter of operational arms control should be examined in greater depth so that it opens up the whole question of developing *counter-strategic* capabilities as part of a wider security policy. This could involve some rather unpalatable and controversial policies which may not yet appear to be fully justified until and unless the exponential growth of nuclear weapon states reaches unacceptable levels, say somewhere around 12 or even fewer.

However, there are a number of disparate issues to be considered, because a world of nuclear powers, above the current modest numbers, would in any event destroy whatever credibility that can still be attached to *collective security* as laid down in Chapter 7 of the UN Charter, *inter alia*. Thus, *collective defence* (Article 51 of the UN Charter), based on self-help, could involve the development of the doctrine of enforced disarmament, which can certainly be justified under existing international law and convention, recognised as pre-emptive strike (self-defence). The logic of this proposition has a national and international dimension in fashioning a new arms control strategy for the twenty-first century. At the alliance level, we should be developing counter-strategic capabilities along the lines of Global Protection against Nuclear Attack (GPALS), an updated defensive missile system for both strategic and tactical defence. At the international level, NATO should over the next 20 years enhance its final resort capability to launch a direct attack against a pariah state's nuclear reactors with Cruise missiles (preferably, where possible, with the putative support and authorisation of the UN Security Council). A defensive ABM capability and an offensive-disarming capacity are different sides of the same coin.

The former policy is clearly *defensive* and the latter policy *offensive* but not *aggressive*, because it involves taking the military initiative to prevent a greater evil, the violation of human rights arising from the use of weapons of mass destruction. At the NATO alliance level, the first type of defensive action involves protecting essential C3i assets and other installations; but with the expansion of the battlefield, cover is likely to prove feasible once updated versions of the Patriot missile or its equivalent become available to NATO.

Clearly, action taken at the international level through calculated pre-emptive action against nuclear installations must take into account the risks involved. An attack on a large, functioning nuclear power reactor would have catastrophic consequences. This option must be one of last desperate resort. The US attacks on Iraq's nuclear facilities during Operation Desert Storm were the first attacks on an operating station. The case of Iraq has greatly legitimised the use of coercive measures against a pariah state through enforced disarmament measures associated with highly intrusive inspection and coercive diplomacy.

Nuclear weapons cannot be disinvented, and therefore, if the international system is to subsist with officially sanctioned nuclear powers, preferably the permanent members of the UN Security Council (UNSC) enjoying a monopoly, then new ground-rules are necessary to guide their conduct. The UNSC and the IAEA must be expected to carry the burden and responsibility for implementing this internationalised nuclear regime for the twenty-first century. A number of crucial issues must be faced. It is clear that the future strategic policy and arms control strategy have to be approached on the basis that we live in a multipolar as well as a multi-nuclear world in which the permanent members of the UNSC – including future members – should have the right to monopolise nuclear weapons as custodians of international security.

There is simply no alternative strategy because a totally nuclear-free world is a chimera, and were it to be achieved it would palpably release pent-up hatreds likely to explode into widespread wars and violence. It is unclear what the nature and extent will be of the contribution to regional collective defence from countries not directly threatened. No one can oblige countries which are not under threat to make more than a symbolic contribution. The nature and extent of such a contribution from these countries will largely be determined on the basis of the national political considerations. This might mean that in some instances a symbolic contribution would be sufficient. There is a risk that unity within NATO could be undermined should countries not react in concert to regional challenges. This problem could be amplified if new members were to be threatened. The geopolitical situation will, however, be more complex than the bipolar world of the Cold War era.

In military terms, the period 1999–2020 will be more like the years between 1815 and 1914 than the years between 1914 and 1990. The North, unless challenged by China or Russia, may therefore be relatively free of great power conflict, but always uneasily co-existing with a world plagued by low-intensity conflicts and social and political upheavals. The developed world will need to cooperate more with other less fortunate countries in order to solve transnational problems such as terrorism, global warming, drugs and debt. The fear of WMD proliferation must, however, be put into its proper perspective.

In a world in which the UNSC's members could attempt to monopolise the possession of nuclear weapons, NATO should make explicit its continued commitment to retaining nuclear weapons as the basis of deterrence. It is NATO's insurance against nuclear attack (and also a counter against missile attacks) or indeed blackmail by rogue states which acquire non-conventional weapons – chemical and biological as well as nuclear. The missile threat to the West is growing with over 20 developing countries currently possessing some ballistic missile capability, some already within range of Europe and, before too long, the United States. Indeed North Korea is within an ace of achieving this. Russia and China are already there.[3]

The Roman dictum, 'If you want peace, prepare for war', must be the watchword for NATO in the twenty-first century. War, not peacekeeping, may yet be in prospect. Against whom? It is not too early to know who will be first to develop the 'electronic battlefield': the Americans will do so. Can others be far behind? NATO–Europe must close the huge technology gap with America if it is to play a part with the United States in global power projection. Such a capability is the essential prerequisite for the maintenance of world order based on a reinvigorated transatlantic relationship.

By 2020, the international system will have changed considerably but *not* beyond recognition. We will still live in a world of nation-states in which any increase in one state's power, no matter how well-motivated, threatens the interests of other states if the norms and values of democratic states are weakened or repudiated. The fundamental nature of international relations has not changed over the millennia. Clearly, international relations continue to be a recurring struggle for wealth and power among independent states living in a near state of nature. We must therefore expect conflict as nation-states and non-state actors multiply and produce conflicting interests.

If the developed world's values are to endure, in the face of the new challenges arising from powerful self-seeking states and messianic groups seeking hegemony, then the West–NATO, the European Union and Japan and, hopefully, a democratic China, must hang together or hang separately.

For the next 20 years, Europe must expect America to lead a more *equal* transatlantic alliance, with due regard to Europe's interests as well as seeking the fulfilment of its own superpower interests. Let us start to prepare for the convergence – economic, political, scientific and technological – of democratic states into a genuine global community capable of defending and sustaining the values of our open, pluralistic societies, the just inheritors of the twenty-first century.

Notes

1 North Atlantic Council Ministers' Meeting, December 1994.
2 A former UNSCOM inspector claims that Iraq has successfully hidden three incomplete nuclear bombs.
3 China has 17-plus intercontinental ballistic missiles (ICBMs) and 70-plus intermediate range ballistic missiles (IRBMs). Russia has 34 nuclear-fuelled ballistic missile submarines (SSBNs) and 800 ICBMs.

6
Development of the Atlantic Relationship: a View from the British Foreign and Commonwealth Office

P. J. Priestley

How did the election of a new British government in 1997 affect the Atlantic relationship? A close relationship with the Clinton Administration was indicated from the start. In the month following the UK election on 1 May 1997, President Clinton visited London, British Foreign Secretary Robin Cook visited Washington and there were any number of transatlantic telephone calls. A month later, the Prime Minister and Foreign Secretary visited Denver for a G8 meeting, where they held bilateral meetings with their US and Canadian opposite numbers. Later in the year, the US Secretary of State, Mrs Albright, and Mr Cook met again in Hong Kong, then in Madrid at a NATO summit and so on and so on.

A healthy transatlantic relationship is a top priority, and of vital importance, to the UK. President Clinton's highly successful visits here have demonstrated the continuing strength of our bilateral relationship with the US. I think it fair to say that the press commentators got it right when they said after the President's first meeting with Mr Blair that with the New Labour government, the relationship had gained a fresh momentum. We aim to keep that up. We remain keen to enhance the relationship by further encouraging close political, commercial and cultural links with the US and Canada. The transatlantic relationship is the bedrock of our security and prosperity. But the world is changing fast. We must not allow the relationship to drift, or to be taken for granted.

The UK has made a major effort to thicken up links between Parliament and Congress. Over 50 members of Congress have visited London for focused discussions on a range of issues. Senator Trent Lott, Senate Majority Leader, led a delegation as early as June 1997. It is reasonable to assume – that is certainly our goal – that every one of these Congressmen will have left these shores with a clearer understanding of our approach to a subject of key importance to them. This is particularly valuable with the younger and newer members who may perhaps have less experience of the international dimensions to the issues in question.

We do not use the term 'special' to describe our relationship with the United States, though I note that the Secretary of State, Madeleine Albright, does. President Clinton has referred to a 'unique partnership', which it certainly is. Whatever term you prefer, the relationship is very close, and in some fields – defence, nuclear, intelligence – it *is* unique. Trade and investment links are vitally important. The UK and the US are the largest single investors in each other's countries. UK/US trade is worth over £42 billion a year (up 12 per cent in 1996), and much more if you include invisibles.

As the Prime Minister and the Foreign Secretary have repeatedly made clear, the government intends to pursue a more constructive relationship with the rest of Europe. But it has also made clear that it sees no contradiction between a Britain that is closely engaged in Europe, and a Europe, including Britain, that maintains a strong alliance and partnership with the United States. If Britain is a leading player in Europe, she is a more valuable ally to the United States.

Mr Blair's excellent relationship with President Clinton will be essential to the success of Britain's foreign policy against a whole range of issues, including global issues such as human rights and environmental protection. The first of these has been most dramatically demonstrated in Yugoslavia.

Close consultation on global issues will also be a feature of our relationship with Canada. We tend to see the world in similar ways. Canada's pioneering work on landmines is one example of where we can work effectively together and where the New Labour government has signalled its desire to play a more active part.

Every so often we hear talk of threats to transatlantic relations from 'Fortress Europe' or of the US looking west to the Pacific rather than east towards Europe. This talk is far from the truth. History and a free trade philosophy have given Britain a global perspective: we cannot accept that Europe should ever be inward-looking. The UK has done much within the EU to promote closer EU/US ties, now formalised in the New Transatlantic Agenda, which provides the framework for cooperation on a range of issues from combating drug-smuggling in the Caribbean to promoting exchanges between our peoples and a forum for business dialogue. There is also close foreign policy cooperation: most notably in the Balkans and also, for example, in the Middle East. During

President Clinton's first visit to Britain, he and the Prime Minister discussed at length the need to work from the Denver G8 meeting onward toward global economic policies which reconcile growth and prosperity with social imperatives, including job creation. We used our presidency of the EU – in the first half of 1998 – to push forward further implementation of the agenda.

There may still be problems in specific sectors, but at least we have a format to keep working on problems and prevent trade disputes turning into trade wars. For example, let us consider our response to the Helms–Burton Act and the D'Amato legislation. We share US concerns about human rights and democracy in Cuba, but we do not accept that extraterritorial trade measures are the right or best way to tackle this. You do not hurt your enemy by hurting your friends. At the moment, Article III of Helms–Burton is suspended. We hope this remains the case.

The most important aspect of the transatlantic relationship, however, is transatlantic *security*. The NATO alliance, which was created in 1949, has provided the most successful and lasting organisation and establishment for peace ever in the world. It has provided and continues to provide peace, stability and security for Europe and the North Atlantic countries.

The present government is fully committed to membership of NATO and its ideals and aims. In his 'Mission Statement' about the aims and objectives of the Foreign and Commonwealth Office, made on 12 May 1997, Mr Cook said 'we shall ensure the security of the United Kingdom and the Dependent Territories and peace for all people by promoting international stability, fostering our defence alliances and promoting arms control actively'. He further went on to say that one of the strategic aims of the United Kingdom's global foreign policy was to make the United Kingdom 'a leading player in a Europe of independent nation states'. He said:

The first goal of foreign policy is security for nations. Security will remain based on the North Atlantic Alliance. We must manage the enlargement of NATO to ensure that a wider alliance is also a stronger alliance and that the process reduces rather than increases tensions between East and West.

Since the end of the Cold War and the disbanding of the former Soviet Union and former Eastern European bloc, there has been considerable movement in Europe and much debate on the process of fundamental political change in NATO itself. In 1997, two years before its fiftieth anniversary, NATO concluded two vitally important agreements: the NATO/Russia Founding Act on Mutual Relations, Co-operation and Security, and the NATO/Ukraine Charter. In addition, NATO established the Euro-Atlantic Partnership Council, which was launched by NATO and partner countries' foreign ministers at the North Atlantic Co-operation Council meeting at Sintra in Portugal that May. At the NATO Summit meeting in Madrid on 8 and 9 July 1997, NATO announced the names of the countries to be invited to join NATO in the fourth enlargement since its inception. Poland, Hungary and the Czech Republic became full members of NATO in March 1999. Britain supported all of these initiatives wholeheartedly.

The NATO/Russia Founding Act on Mutual Relations, Co-operation and Security

The Act was signed by NATO heads of state and government, including our own Prime Minister and President Clinton, the NATO Secretary-General and President Yeltsin at a NATO/Russia Summit in Paris on 27 May 1997. It represented an historic breakthrough in relations between Russia and the West. The Founding Act provided for a list of shared principles including the right of states to choose the means to ensure their own security. It introduced arrangements for a permanent joint council which, that autumn, began meeting monthly at ambassadorial level, twice-yearly at Ministerial level and on demand in a crisis. This is probably the jewel in the crown. It provides, if Russia takes full advantage of its opportunities, the basis for an improved relationship between Russia and the West, based on mutual trust and the aim of security in Europe.

The Founding Act also provided a full list of subjects for consultation and cooperation, including security crises, crisis management and conflict resolution, joint operations, defence policy and military doctrine, arms control, nuclear weapons and doctrine and more. There is a section on military issues, including restatements of previous unilateral statements by NATO on its nuclear and conventional force deployments, and an agreed approach to CFE adaptation and provisions for more cooperation between military establishments.

There have been critics of the Founding Act. One of two principal criticisms is that it will undermine NATO. Our answer to that is that, to the extent that Russia is prepared to use the Joint Council constructively, her voice will be heard more clearly by NATO. This is in the West's interests. We accept that Russia has a genuine security preoccupation.

The second criticism is that the agreement will undermine Russia, and especially the Russian leadership, in the eyes of their people. Our response to that is that closer cooperation between Russia and the West will help clearer understanding and help the view of NATO as a bogey-man disappear from the eyes of the Russian people.

The NATO/Ukraine Charter

Shortly after concluding the NATO/Russia Founding Act, NATO Foreign Ministers initialled a Charter with the Ukraine on 29 May 1997. We particularly welcomed this special arrangement. The UK has been a strong partner of Ukraine since its independence. We have supported its efforts to map out a new strategic position in Europe, to develop links with the West while trying to resolve outstanding disputes with Russia over the Black Sea fleet and Crimea. We hope that they will continue to use to the full the practical NATO mechanisms for cooperation. Ukraine has, of course, a special status in its relationship with Russia, together with being a member of the Euro-Atlantic Partnership Council. The Charter takes account of Ukraine's individual security needs and allows scope for NATO and Ukraine to develop cooperation in a dynamic process. However, we realise the need for a balanced relationship between Russia and NATO.

The Euro-Atlantic Partnership Council and the Enhanced Partnership for Peace

In another development, the day after the NATO/Ukraine Charter was initialled, the Council established with its partners the Euro-Atlantic Partnership Council (EAPC), which takes the place of the North Atlantic Co-operation Council (NACC). The EAPC provides a new more cohesive institutional framework for cooperation between the 19 Allies and 24 partner countries. It integrates activities previously pursued separately in the NACC and the Partnership for Peace programme (PfP). Ministers at their Sintra meeting also approved a report on enhanced PfP (PfP+) which will retain its 'brand name' under the EAPC.

Work on the EAPC/PfP+ package was guided by three over-arching aims:

- to strengthen the political consultation element in PfP;
- to develop a more operational role for PfP;
- to provide for greater involvement of partners in PfP decision-making and planning.

The North Atlantic Co-operation Council was inaugurated in 1991 with the aim of providing help to partner nations in security-related areas during the post-Cold War transition process. It laid the groundwork for the PfP programme subsequently launched at the NATO Summit in January 1994. Since then the relevance of the annual NACC Ministerial meetings and their separate programmes has waned. It will be replaced by the EAPC.

The EAPC will meet bi-annually at defence and foreign minister level and monthly at ambassadorial level. It will be able to meet in plenary session with all 43 members, in smaller open-ended groups or in the 19-allies-plus-one-partner format. This arrangement whereby one partner or a group of partners can consult individually with all 19 allies is especially useful in building partner members' confidence in security.

All meetings of the EAPC are chaired by NATO's Secretary-General or his deputy, although a representative of a partner country will be named honorary president. The EAPC is be supported by NATO committees meeting with representatives of partners.

The mandate of the EAPC is not defined in the basic document, although there is an indicative list of possible subjects for consultation. This reflects the desire at this stage to retain maximum flexibility in format and scope. Much of its success will depend on how cooperation between Allies and the partners develops in practice and how much substance this will provide to the political dimension of the partnership.

Partnership for Peace (PfP)

The Partnership for Peace has in little more than two years developed into an intensive programme of practical defence and military cooperation. It has the following aims:

1 advising partners on the process of the reform of their defence and military structures (for example democratic civilian control of armed forces, budgetary transparency, cost-effectiveness), thus transparency and confidence in security matters among members;
2 developing the capabilities of partners' armed forces to cooperate with NATO forces (for example in peace-keeping) and by joint exercising and increasing inter-operability;
3 projecting stability through the 'soft' security of NATO's commitment to consultation in the event that a partner perceives a threat to its territorial integrity, political independence or security.

The enhanced Partnership for Peace was agreed by Ministers when the EAPC was established. The aims of the EAPC and PfP+ are:

1   to provide an expanded political dimension to the partnership, greater cohesion for NATO's outreach activities in the political, defence and military areas and a substantially higher level of practical cooperation; and

2   to involve partners in PfP planning and decision-making and further opening NATO committees and activities to bring allies and partners together on a more equal footing.

The EAPC/PfP gives the partnership a new start. It has more political visibility, wider practical cooperation, more equality between Allies and partners and more access by partners to NATO. In addition, it will provide a long-term framework for cooperation, not just a waiting room for NATO membership. The EAPC is likely to become the mechanism through which all NATO-led peace support operations will be co-ordinated.

It is now up to partners and allies to give substance to these arrangements. Two important principles will be retained: inclusiveness (EAPC and PfP+ will be open to all partners and allies equally) and self-differentiation (partners will continue to be able to decide for themselves the level and areas of cooperation in which they wish to be involved).

Britain has been active in NATO's work on a strengthened package of arrangements under PfP, including more involvement for partners in decision-making: more political consultations; a wider range of military cooperation to include peace support operations; partner involvement with NATO headquarters and with Combined Joint Task Forces (CJTFs). The EAPC in essence repackages this substance in a politically eye-catching structure.

NATO enlargement

One of the most exciting and controversial questions which NATO addressed in recent years was the prospect of a fourth enlargement of the alliance, to which all members were committed. There were twelve aspirants applying to join the alliance in 1997. The argument basically centred on whether a first wave of new membership should consist of three or five. It was generally recognised in NATO that there were only five credible candidates at the time. The United States had already announced that it would support a smaller wave consisting of Poland, Hungary and the Czech Republic. The other two 'short-listed' candidates, Romania and Slovenia, also lobbied hard for inclusion. Britain decided to support the smaller wave only immediately prior to the July

1997 Madrid summit of the alliance where the decision was to be announced. The guiding principles of membership were that new members should contribute to a full range of alliance missions and increase security of the alliance as a whole.

Failure to be invited to negotiate admission in Madrid was not, however, the end of the story. NATO foreign ministers had pledged that the alliance would remain open to the accession of further members in accordance with Article 10 of the Washington Treaty, and NATO was determined that admission of new members must not mean less security for those not invited or that new dividing lines should be created in Europe. The UK remains committed to NATO's work to broaden and deepen the military and political dimensions of Partnership for Peace. This will play an integral part in Europe's security architecture and is not a consolation prize for those countries who were not invited to join.

One of the criticisms of NATO enlargement was that a large and adapted NATO would be a diluted NATO. The UK disputed this. An enlarged and adapted NATO has an enhanced ability to meet the diverse challenges of the post-Cold War world, but it must also remain an effective military alliance for collective defence under Article 5 of the Washington Treaty.

A second criticism was that NATO enlargement would threaten Russia. The NATO/Russia Founding Act has as its centrepiece the NATO/Russia Council, which will build confidence and understanding on security issues. We understand Russia's security concerns and do not ignore them. NATO needs a close and trusting relationship with Russia. NATO enlargement does not threaten this.

There was also some concern, both publicly and in Parliament in Britain, about the cost of NATO enlargement. It was not been possible to make estimates in advance. Although some work was done in NATO, costs depended on which countries joined NATO, when and on what terms. These costs, which fall on both countries which join and on existing members of the alliance, are being incurred over a long period. Subject to the two preceding caveats, we expect the costs of enlargement will turn out to be manageable.

The Madrid Summit

The 1997 Madrid Summit, which was attended by heads of state and government, had a lot of far-reaching decisions to take. In addition to those I described earlier, there were the questions of the Command Structure Review, of a European Security and Defence Identity (ESDI) and of CJTFs. On the Command Structure Review there is an emerging consensus on the broad shape of the higher levels of the new Command Structure. But for most nations including Britain, much depends on how this is fleshed out in detail. Ministers have agreed the working assumptions that there should continue to be two United States-led Strategic Commands and that there should be three rather than the existing four levels of command. Ministers have agreed on a three-region structure in the Atlantic and selected two models for the future European structure, one based on two regional commands and the other based on three. Britain wishes to see a new Command Structure, which is militarily effective and cost-efficient, but we will need clear assurances on resource/manpower implications and the operational effectiveness of a new structure.

ESDI

The development of a European Security and Defence Identity (ESDI) within NATO should allow European allies to have the ability to undertake smaller-scale non-Article 5 operations, in which the US might not wish to take part. The role of the Western European Union (WEU) is being built up to allow it to provide political control of European operations, and linked to this is work under way to make NATO assets – including combined Joint Task Forces Headquarters – available to the WEU. France in particular is concerned for an increased European representation in the command structure as a condition for her re-entry into NATO's military structure. That said, we believe that good progress has been made on developing ESDI within NATO, and strengthening links with the WEU.

Combined Joint Task Forces (CJTFs)

One objective of the Command Structure Review has been to create savings through a reduction in fixed headquarters to fund the creation of Combined Joint Task Forces (CJTFs) to allow NATO to respond more effectively to new-style missions it is likely to undertake. A CJTF is a nucleus headquarters, which in a crisis would be augmented in a manner tailored to the operation and then deployed as a theatre command HQ. We have taken the view that because of resource implications, NATO is unlikely to be able to afford more than two effective European-based CJTFs (Brunssum and Naples). A number of smaller nations, however, are continuing to argue for smaller CJTF headquarters on their territory. We welcome the real progress being made on implementing the CJTF concept. It is very important in providing NATO with the capability it will need to deal with likely future tasks.

Conclusion

From the above I hope the reader will conclude that Britain is fully committed to the future of NATO and to the diverse and blooming Atlantic relationship. As Prime Minister Tony Blair said in Paris following the signature of the NATO/Russia Founding Act on 27 May 1997, 'Mine is the first generation able to contemplate the possibility that we may live our entire lives without going to war or sending our children to war. This is a prize beyond value and this agreement is a great contribution.' He continued, 'NATO has served my country well. It has served Europe well. It remains the cornerstone of Europe's defence.'

7
The Politics of Trade in an Ever-Closer Community

Don E. Newquist

This chapter is concerned with some elements of trade policy that are particularly relevant in the light of NATO and EU expansion. First, we have witnessed both notable failures and notable successes in recent EU–US trade relations. These items clearly demonstrate the challenges of an ambitious policy. Next, agriculture remains a lingering problem and several pertinent issues will be magnified by a potential EU expansion. Finally, I would like to discuss how we measure the success of trade initiatives and policies. This is especially relevant at this time.

The European Union and the United States share a unique relationship which I do not need to describe in depth here; but, a few points help to establish the dimensions of our relationship. The US and the EU together account for one-half of world trade. The EU is the largest market for US exports, accounting for almost one-half of the exports of US firms and amounting to over $1 trillion in sales. And this trade is balanced: trade surpluses and deficits of the United States with Europe have netted out almost to zero historically.

This mutually beneficial relationship has thrived because of the far-sighted policy of integration and free trade that the governments in the EU and US have pursued. The United States has long supported initiatives to achieve greater political and economic unity among European nations. Greater political and economic unity in Europe have been in our own self-interest. A politically united Europe is a strong partner in the advancement of common goals. An economically united Europe creates a much more attractive environment for American investment. Furthermore, a common currency that cements an open single market and sparks economic growth in Europe can provide expansive opportunities for American businesses.

The EU and the US have also worked together to liberalise world trade. Every advance in the world trading system since the Bretton Woods conference in 1944 has been the result of agreement and action that the European Union (and its predecessors) and the United States have taken together.

Likewise, the expansion of NATO can create an environment which, because it is more stable and peaceful, will be conducive to the European Union's expansion eastward. Many of Europe's new democracies are well on their way to meeting the economic conditions for EU membership. But EU governments and Western investors must also be confident about the long-term, deep-seated security of the region, and that is what NATO can provide.

Our regional trading systems, the EU and NAFTA, are springboards for changing and expanding global commerce. The EU of the twenty-first century, with around 25 countries, some of them sharing a single currency and some with only a recent experience of market economics, is bound to be different. The North American Free Trade Agreement (NAFTA), too, can become more integrated and larger in the coming decade.

Over the last 50 years, the relationship between the EU (and its forerunners) and the US has been highlighted by an unmistakable trend towards open markets and free trade. Generally speaking, the EU and US have chosen the high road of free trade over the narrow politics of domestic protection. But, as the history of the EU shows, the road to an 'Ever-Closer Community' has not always been without skirmishes. So too, the effort to expand the commercial ties between the EU and US has sometimes fallen victim to domestic interests.

Often, these problems are the result of disagreements that have occurred in the absence of any normative rules. When we have had a clear rules structure, the decision-making agencies have been able to adjudicate in an environment free from the shadow of political pressures, just as we are now seeing the orderly resolution of disputes brought about by the improved dispute settlement mechanism of the World Trade Organisation. But, until we have a clear policy and a predictable process, the concept of free trade can continue to fall victim to domestic political pressures.

I would like briefly to touch on some current issues that highlight the challenges of ever closer relations, yet still demonstrate the commitment to such relations. While the EU and the US share a mutually beneficial relationship and a common interest in world trade, that fact does not mean that their views always coincide. In my experience, a lack of attention to details by governments has led to many disputes, some of which have come before the USITC.

Take, for example, that most American of foods, the French fry. NAFTA has thrown open a lot of doors, and, in many ways, has created a single French fry market in North America. Commercial relations are especially close between the US and Canada, and developed as a result of the United States–Canada free trade agreement enacted several years before NAFTA. As the market has developed, many parts of the Eastern United States are now supplied with French fries produced in Eastern Canada. In the West, it is the other way around. If it makes economic sense, that is the way it should be.

But there are problems. US farmers do not like to hear that people in Boston or New York are eating Canadian potatoes when Maine potatoes are rotting in their fields. Many of the complaints raised by US farmers concerned subsidies by the Canadian government to the potato industry. This is where the NAFTA governments have neglected to look after the details of the Agreement. They have not moved on to the hard work that NAFTA requires to harmonise the subsidies that each government provides to its domestic firms. In this sense, NAFTA is years behind the EU in reconciling these government programmes.

In EU–US trade, the Boeing–McDonnell Douglas merger provides a good example of domestic political posturing obscuring the goal of free trade. The objections of the EU Commission to the merger were that it would create a virtual monopoly, that exclusive contracts of Boeing with Continental, American and Delta were unfair, and that Boeing might benefit from research and development subsidies given to McDonnell Douglas. The EU Competition Commissioner threatened fines of more than $4 billion in order to hold off the merger until changes in its terms could be negotiated.

The European Commission's concerns may have been valid, but it is not my intention to analyse their merits. Instead, I want to point out how our countries reached this situation and what it tells us about the challenges of structuring free trade initiatives.

First, the absence of a defined procedure for analysing mergers deposited this transaction in the political arena. While there is a 1991 cooperation agreement which laid down guidelines for 'comity' between the EU and the United States in competition investigations, this agreement only sets guidelines for how the governments should get along. It does not formally restrict either side from doing whatever it wants.

Second, the EU policy of protecting Airbus (which must be regarded as a 'European' company) at the expense of free trade looks to be a significant detractor from transatlantic relations. There is an even larger issue here than the mere protection of a domestic industry: the consequences of government interference with the dynamic creative process by which entrepreneurs flourish. World competition should spark new markets and new challenges. Through diligence and perseverance, Boeing and Airbus have captured 95 per cent of the world market and seem to be tireless competitors in a healthy economic fight. This represents the success of the industry.

But there is a down side. In this race for markets, governments have been dragged into the commercial battles, and policies have been altered in the interest of each company. Some would say that in negotiations with other countries our governments have been played off against each other to get the best deal.

If we fail to anticipate and provide a means for accommodating new business relationships that emerge from global marketing successes, we risk the undisputed benefits of free and open trade. Thus, perhaps this disagreement demonstrates the need for the globalisation of competition policy, which creates an open environment for trade and removes governments from what should be private commercial matters. In this sense, when the EU and US focus on our common interest, the goals we achieve are impressive, such as the Uruguay Round and the creation of the World Trade Organization. It is in our common interest to learn from this dispute and to work to harmonise competition policy in the global community. Such an agreement would help limit the distractions of politics and avoid the needless derailment of future integration efforts.

A good example of the future potential for integration and a model for how we should look to expand our relationships are the recently implemented Mutual Recognition Agreements (MRAs). The business community, as represented by the Trans-Atlantic Business Dialogue (TABD), has long considered standards to be a major concern. The MRAs make it possible for a US exporter to have its products undergo various conformity-assessment procedures in the US according to EU requirements, and for EU producers to do the same in the EU for products bound for the US. This will reduce the cost of product testing and inspection on over $50 billion in bilateral trade, and could save almost $175 million a year in legal and bureaucratic costs.

In our work at the United States International Trade Commission, the issue of standards has been raised repeatedly in the context of our relations with Canada, and even with regard to Mexico under NAFTA. The fact that the US and the EU have been able to reach an agreement in this area that greatly facilitates trade between them is indicative of the strength of the transatlantic relationship.

While the successful agreement is impressive, hard work still remains to be done. For example, the MRAs do not cover automobiles, and it will take long and diligent work to overcome the political opposition to automobile standards. EU member states still have widely differing standards, testing and certification procedures in place for some products. Such differences, while not deliberate 'trade barriers', are impediments to the free movement of products and have caused delays in sales due to product-testing and certification requirements to meet differing national standards. Hopefully, the 'New Approach' will lead to the harmonisation of laws, regulations, standards, testing, quality and certification procedures in the EU.

I point out these problems not to cast blame, but to demonstrate that while the headline-grabbing Mutual Recognition Agreements are a good and insightful beginning, only the difficult and complicated negotiations to follow will create the true and lasting achievement.

There have been other recent agreements that have helped to create a free and fair business environment. Thirty-nine countries accounting for 92.3 per cent of world trade in information technology products signed the landmark Information Technology Agreement (ITA). At no time in the history of the trading system have so many countries united to open up trade in a single sector by eliminating duties across the board. This agreement, combined with the recent Agreement on Telecommunications Services, has established a solid foundation for the global economic infrastructure needed for trade expansion as we look to the next century. Also, the OECD agreed to outlaw the bribery of foreign officials. This pact is the first global accord making it a crime to bribe foreign officials to obtain contracts, and will help create a more transparent business environment.

Accession of new members to the EU means that the US will face a stronger, larger, more competitive Europe. But stronger income growth and increased economic activity historically also mean increased opportunities for trade for businesses both in the EU and the US.

In view of the potential expansion of the EU, we must continue to find areas of agreement and to conclude difficult and complicated negotiations despite political concerns. One such area is agricultural policy, which has remained hostage to domestic concerns and continues to be the most contentious issue between the US and EU. While the accession of new members to the EU will create new challenges in EU–US agricultural policy, it could also be the means necessary to finally reach mutually satisfactory agreements to problems that have long plagued trade in this sector. The US undoubtedly has a strong agricultural sector. Being from Texas, and having grown up in a farming community, I know how vital agriculture is to the US and I can appreciate the concern felt in Europe for Europe's farmers.

There are a number of issues which currently complicate trade in agriculture between the EU and US. Several aspects of the Common Agricultural Policy (CAP) have long irritated agricultural interests in the United States in their efforts to gain access to the EU market and to compete with EU producers in the world market. EU export subsidies (restitutions) on a wide range of agricultural products including wheat, wheat flour, beef, dairy products, poultry, and certain fruits, as well as some manufactured products such as pasta, have disrupted world markets. The EU ban on the importation of animals, and meat from animals, which have been administered any of six particular hormones is viewed by farmers in the US as a protectionist measure. Scientists have reviewed these hormones and concluded that they are safe in normal use, and the EU permits some of these same hormones to be administered for herd-management and other purposes. The EU has been slow to abide by the decision of the World Trade Organisation panel that ruled against the import ban on these products.

In preparation for accession to the EU, the countries of Central and Eastern Europe have signed association agreements with the EU and announced their intention to align their agricultural policies with the Common Agricultural Policy. These countries produce significant quantities of grains, meats and milk, and their production potential appears much larger than their current output. That these countries seem to be moving toward protectionism in the region, by establishing guaranteed minimum prices to growers for selected products and imposing high border protection measures, is troubling.

The potential accession of Central and Eastern European countries to the EU highlights problems already present in the current EU structure. Even in the absence of accession, there are concerns about the extent to which the EU will be able to comply with its Uruguay Round commitments under current CAP policies. Membership of the large agricultural producing countries of Central and Eastern Europe would appear to create serious problems for the CAP in its current form, and would impose major strains on EU budgets, including the agricultural budget under the CAP as it currently operates.

Some are now concerned that this process will result in additional trade problems. Production by the countries of Central and Eastern

Europe could significantly increase under the current price and income support mechanisms of the CAP. Already, under the contemporary association agreements, the EU has provided a greater degree of access for these countries, which has led to a decrease of NAFTA-origin agricultural imports. Furthermore, extending the CAP to Central and Eastern European countries would also offer those farmers a far greater incentive to produce than under their current system. This is a major concern for the NAFTA countries since this would likely add to EU surpluses in grains and livestock products. Within the EU, however, lower production costs in the Central and Eastern European countries for these products, as well as for fruits and vegetables, are also seen as a threat to EU farmers, who produce at a higher cost.

In the light of these changes, the time may be ripe for a major re-evaluation of agricultural trade relations between the EU and US and for pursuing a policy that continues to look outward rather than inward. The next round of multilateral agricultural negotiations scheduled to begin in the World Trade Organisation in 2000 will provide a prime opportunity for such a re-evaluation.

Agricultural supports create domestic distortions, and also have international effects in terms of lower world market prices. Acting together to reduce trade-distorting support measures will ease the adjustment as well as reduce the political pressures. Consequently, only if the NAFTA countries and the EU work together can we eliminate trade-distorting subsidies. Especially in agriculture, the transition period may be slow, difficult, and imperfect. This is why we have the safeguard provisions, and they must work. But, existence of safeguard provisions does not mean we have abandoned the policy of free trade. Hopefully, a comprehensive adjustment of agricultural trade policy between the EU and US, including the necessary safeguard provisions, will be possible in light of the potential challenges posed by further accession to the EU.

In planning new agreements and addressing existing trade problems we also need to remain cognisant of how the public relates to the development of free trade policies and how we measure the success of these policies. The International Trade Commission recently finished a confidential assessment of NAFTA prepared for the United States Trade Representative. The results of that study are not the topic of this discussion, but one of the major issues that emerged has quite a bit of relevance here. In the course of the study we came to realise just how many people in the USA view free trade with a lot of suspicion. I notice that many of Europe's people seem similarly disillusioned with some of the regional integration policies in Europe.

In the hearings that we held in conjunction with the NAFTA study, economists and business people appeared before the Commission and, one after another, said that NAFTA has had a modest, positive effect. Yet, Congress and the President refuse to touch the issue right now. Politicians are cognisant of the perception that free trade causes somebody to lose. I am sure that Europeans have plenty of experience with politicians using trade issues against their opponents to win elections. Free trade, it seems, can easily be hijacked for narrow political purposes. Sometimes you do make sacrifices to domestic interests, but ultimately the policy that we have been pursuing is the correct one: more free trade, more integration.

We must work to create an environment where business can succeed on its own merits rather than through the threats and exhortations of governments involved. The United States and the European Union have worked hard to move toward a policy of free trade, and in recent years have produced results. The EU and US must cooperate to bring China, Russia and other countries into the rules-based system of the WTO. Encouraging countries to abide by the rules of international organisations like the WTO, like NATO and like the EU encourages commerce to develop in more predictable patterns and removes the narrow domestic attitudes that are so often pervasive.

The New Trans-Atlantic Agenda (NTAA) has developed an ambitious agenda for expanding cooperation between the US and EU by promoting peace and democracy and expanding trade and contacts between our societies. The Trans-Atlantic Business Dialogue (TABD) helps our business communities find common ground to remove barriers to commerce and fair trade. The TABD provides a productive way for business and government to work together. The recently agreed Transatlantic Economic Partnership has an action plan that involves extended coverage of the Mutual Recognition Agreements, closer cooperation between regulators across the Atlantic, further liberalisation in government procurement and intellectual property protection, and cooperation on health and environmental issues.

These institutions are valuable assets in achieving the goal of a barrier-free transatlantic marketplace. We should strive to build these institutions which expand and strengthen the network of connections and associations, and which enable us to find common ground for agreement, to transcend the short-term politics of closed markets. Institutions such as the EU and NAFTA foster attitudes that make a global community an eventual reality. Whatever we do to strengthen and expand them can only help accomplish this goal.

With regard to trade policy in general, but especially with regard to agriculture, the costs of adjustment are painfully apparent to both producers and employees in the affected industries. In contrast, the benefits are broadcast throughout the economy, primarily to consumers, who in most cases may not realise the benefits they are deriving from the trade liberalisation. In the long run, it is difficult to quantify trade benefits to show the success of a certain policy. Sometimes, the true benefit may be intangible, such as a more predictable environment for business risk. I know that in the United States there will be some who wonder why we need to care at all about Hungary or Malta or Cyprus. Thus, I think the basis of our future relationship depends on our ability to educate and inform people so that they know of the benefits of free trade and why we continue to pursue it, notwithstanding the successes and failures of our past efforts at economic integration.

8
Trade Developments in the Western Hemisphere: Implications for Transatlantic Relations

Joseph A. McKinney

The transatlantic relationship is affected in important ways not only by issues of direct and immediate concern to the major parties, but also by regional developments that have an indirect bearing on the relationship. This article focuses on recent developments within the Western Hemisphere, specifically those relating to international trade and regional economic integration, and ways in which they may affect transatlantic relations.

Background

From the formation of the General Agreement on Tariffs and Trade until the mid-1980s, the United States adhered faithfully to the most-favoured-nation principle of non-discrimination in international trade. An important shift in this policy occurred with trade legislation in 1984 which authorised a free trade agreement with Israel and opened the door to subsequent agreements with other countries. In 1985 Canada, the largest trading partner of the United States, also requested free trade negotiations. The agreement with Canada became effective in 1989, and the next year Mexico requested a free trade agreement. After protracted negotiations and the required parliamentary approvals, the North American free trade agreement (NAFTA) took effect on 1 January 1994.

Merely a decade earlier, such an agreement would have been considered highly improbable. Both of the North American neighbours of the United States have historically resisted economic domination by the large and powerful nation next door, and have taken care to keep the United States at arm's length. As protectionist sentiment grew in the United States during the mid-1980s, however, Canada decided that secure access to its most important market was worth relinquishing some of its economic independence. A few years later, Mexico, which had by that time embarked upon an ambitious economic reform programme, concluded that its best hope of attracting sorely needed investment capital was also to establish secure access to the United States market through a free trade agreement. None of the countries of North America had any interest in establishing regional supranational institutions that might infringe upon their sovereignty. Indeed, each country insisted upon maintaining its separate extra-regional trade policy as well as its own set of domestic economic policies.

The effects of the NAFTA agreement were felt even before it entered into force. During the four years leading up to its implementation, trade among the three countries of North America expanded rapidly. That trend continued during 1994 as the agreed tariff reductions began to take effect. In December of that year the heads of state of 34 American republics met in Miami for a Summit of the Americas and agreed in principle to negotiate a Free Trade Area for the Americas which would include all of the democracies of the Western Hemisphere by the year 2005. Chile had already requested accession to NAFTA, and other countries in the hemisphere were expected soon to follow suit.

Only a few weeks later, however, Mexico suffered a collapse of its currency's value. This peso crisis led to a severe contraction of the Mexican economy. A spillover effect was felt throughout Latin America as capital flows to the region decreased and the currencies of several Latin American countries came under extreme pressure. The United States was affected as well, not so much by the economic effects of the peso crisis as from the psychological impact which caused many in the country to question the stability of Latin American economies and the wisdom of linking too closely with them. Prospects for Western Hemispheric free trade were dealt a serious blow by the economic difficulties of Mexico.

Viewed in terms of its economic effects, the NAFTA agreement must be judged a success thus far despite Mexico's currency crisis. Trade among the three countries of North America has continued to expand rapidly. The United States now trades more with Canada than with all 15 countries of the European Union combined, and Mexico in 1997 replaced Japan as the second largest export market of the United States. Largely because of NAFTA, Mexico's economic reform process has remained intact and has even been deepened to some extent during a time of extreme economic hardship. Mexican industrial production, led by a surge of exports to the United States, recovered its pre-crisis level in less than one-half the time that was required after the peso crisis of 1982. Direct foreign investment flows into Mexico, which in the peso crisis of the 1980s dropped precipitously, were almost double during 1994–96 what they had been during the three years immediately preceding NAFTA.[1] The assured market access and investor confidence provided by the codified rules of NAFTA most certainly contributed to the rapid economic recovery of Mexico after its latest currency crisis.

While having NAFTA in place has greatly benefited Mexico during its time of economic crisis, this benefit has not been at the expense of the other NAFTA countries. Despite fears that the agreement would cause unemployment in the United States, during its first three years the United States economy generated a net increase of over 8 million jobs and the rate of unemployment decreased by nearly 2 per cent. Canada's economic performance has likewise been impressive since NAFTA has been in effect.

Nevertheless, the impetus toward a Free Trade Area for the Americas was definitely diminished by the peso crisis. Environmental and labour groups that had opposed NAFTA succeeded in linking the peso crisis to NAFTA in the minds of the public, and used Mexico's economic difficulties as an argument against expansion of free trade throughout the hemisphere. Because of what Richard Feinberg has termed 'an unholy alliance between right-wing nationalist Republicans and union-financed liberal Democrats', a deadlock developed within the United States Congress over the terms under which the necessary fast-track legislation for meaningful hemispheric trade negotiations might be extended.[2] The major dispute concerns whether trade sanctions should be available to enforce minimum environmental and labour standards throughout the hemisphere. The Democrats in Congress insist as a condition of their support for fast track that trade sanctions be included in the legislation as an enforcement mechanism. The Republican majority in Congress insist that the absence of trade sanctions is a necessary condition for their support of fast-track legislation.

The issues that have stymied progress toward a Free Trade Area for the Americas in the United States Congress are by no means limited in their scope only to the countries of the Western Hemisphere. They reflect broader concerns about the societal effects of globalisation. Rapid economic changes are requiring tremendous adjustments in many industries, increasing the demand for skilled workers and reducing the demand for those with lower skills. In the United States, these changes have created a widened gap between the wages of skilled and unskilled workers. In the less flexible labour markets of Western Europe the same phenomena have been responsible for an increased rate of unemployment.[3] Although the weight of empirical evidence points to technological change as the primary cause of these developments, a deep suspicion remains on the part of many that increased trade with labour-abundant countries is responsible.[4] This has caused reluctance on the part of labour interests in the more economically developed countries to enter into new trade agreements without some protections for workers. Trade sanctions are said to be necessary to convince low-wage countries to upgrade their labour standards and labour practices.

Some environmental groups also have been vocal and effective in their opposition to free trade agreements that include less developed countries, with their lower environmental standards. These groups fear that through an unfair cost advantage, arising from less stringent environmental standards, the less developed countries will attract industries from, and increase their product market share at the expense of, more developed countries which maintain higher environmental standards. This, it is said, may lead to a 'race to the bottom' in which countries compete to gain competitive advantage through degrading their environmental standards.[5]

No convincing evidence exists that a 'race to the bottom' has ever occurred, or is likely to occur. Theoretically, currency values should adjust to offset any hypothetical advantage that a country might gain from lower environmental standards.[6] Nevertheless, many environmentalists remain unconvinced, and environmental non-governmental organisations (NGOs) have been quite effective in expressing their opposition to trade agreements. The fact that the Committee on Trade and Environment of the World Trade Organisation has been slow to address concerns of environmentalists has exacerbated this situation.

Trade developments within the Western Hemisphere

The Summit of the Americas, which was held in Miami in December 1994, issued a Declaration of Principles which was very ambitious and broad in scope. Special note was taken of the fact that, for the first time in history, the countries of the Western Hemisphere (excepting Cuba) were a community of democratic societies. And despite many differences in cultures and levels of economic development, the countries of the hemisphere were united in their commitment to economic progress through open markets and economic integration. The Declaration of Principles articulated four main goals: to preserve and strengthen the community of democracies of the Americas; to promote prosperity through economic integration and free trade; to eradicate poverty and discrimination in the hemisphere; and to guarantee sustainable development and conserve the natural environment for future generations. The Plan of Action which accompanied the Declaration of Principles contained more than 150 action items.

At the time these plans were laid, the clear expectation was that the United States would take the lead in the negotiations for a Free Trade Area for the Americas. That has not happened. However, even though the Clinton administration has thus far been unable to obtain fast-track

Table 8.1 FTAA time line

Date	Event
9–11 December 1994	At Summit of the Americas, leaders of the 34 democratically elected heads of state of the Western Hemisphere agree to begin immediately to construct the Free Trade Area for the Americas (FTAA) in which barriers to trade and investment will be progressively eliminated.
30 June 1995	At first trade ministerial meeting at Denver, Colorado, ministers issue a joint declaration and initial a work programme for creating a hemispheric free trade zone by 2005. The ministers agreed that the FTAA would be fully consistent with the World Trade Organisation, be balanced and comprehensive in scope, and represent a single undertaking comprising mutual rights and obligations. Seven working groups were established.
21 March 1996	Meeting in Cartagena, Colombia, FTAA trade ministers agree to establish an additional four working groups.
13–16 May 1997	Third FTAA Trade Ministerial held in Belo Horizonte, Brazil. Among other things, the ministers commit to formally launch FTAA negotiations at the April 1998 Summit of the Americas and that consensus would be the basis of decision-making in the FTAA.
1 June 1997	First Preparatory Committee meeting results in approval of the agenda to be negotiated for the 1998 Summit including a US-proposed reference to labour standards.
17 March 1998	Fourth FTAA Preparatory Committee meeting held in San Jose, Costa Rica. Agreement reached on the structure, organisation and venue for FTAA negotiations. A Trade Negotiations Committee was established to oversee the negotiations, meeting twice a year beginning on 30 June 1998. Nine negotiating groups were established.

Source: United States International Trade Commission, *International Economic Review*, USITC Publication 3109, March/April/May 1998.

negotiating authority for a Free Trade Area for the Americas, a number of preliminary steps toward such an agreement have been taken (see Table 8.1).

Since the First Summit of the Americas was held in Miami in 1994, the hemispheric trade ministers have met once a year to consider how best to implement the plans for hemispheric free trade. A dozen working groups have been established to provide the background information that will eventually be needed for free trade negotiations.[7] These working groups have compiled inventories of trading practices throughout the hemisphere. Much of this information had never been gathered before, and it was essential preparation for the eventual negotiations.

At the Denver trade ministerial meeting in 1995, agreement was reached that the Free Trade Area for the Americas would be a 'single undertaking'. This was interpreted by the United States to mean that all of the countries involved would eventually assume all of the obligations of the agreement, i.e., that there would be no 'free riders'. Brazil and some other Latin American countries interpreted the terminology to mean that the entire free trade agreement would be negotiated before any of its provisions took effect.

At the 1997 trade ministerial meeting, strong differences of opinion emerged between Brazil and the United States concerning how the eventual free trade negotiations should proceed. The United States proposed talks on market-access issues from the beginning, whereas Brazil proposed focusing first on business facilitation measures such as standardising trade documentation, with market-access issues postponed until two years later. The United States had hoped to press for an 'early harvest' of agreement on issues such as market access, investment regulations, government procurement procedures, and intellectual property issues. The lack of fast-track negotiating authority has weakened the United States' leadership in the process, however, and it has had to settle for early agreement only on certain business facilitation measures. Implementation of all other measures will have to wait until the conclusion of the negotiations.

At the 1998 hemispheric trade ministerial meeting in San Jose, Costa Rica, agreement was reached to begin formal Free Trade Area for the Americas negotiations in Miami no later than September 1998. Nine negotiating groups were specified, along with a chair and vice-chair for each (see Table 8.2). Responsibilities for chairing the negotiating groups was shared among many countries, with the experts from the Inter-American Development Bank, Organisation of American States and

Table 8.2 FTAA negotiating groups with designated chairs and vice-chairs

Negotiating group	Chair	Vice-chair
Market Access	Colombia	Bolivia
Investment	Costa Rica	Dominican Republic
Services	Nicaragua	Barbados
Government Procurement	United States	Honduras
Dispute Settlement	Chile	Uruguay-Paraguay
Agriculture	Argentina	El Salvador
Intellectual Property Rights	Venezuela	Ecuador
Subsidies, AD/CVD	Brazil	Chile
Competition Policy	Peru	Trinidad and Tobago

United Nations Economic Commission for Latin America and the Caribbean available to provide advice and technical support as needed.

The list of negotiating groups makes it apparent that the proposed Free Trade Area of the Americas will involve much more than a conventional free trade area which would remove import tariffs among the members. Many of the negotiating issues involve the deeper integration measures that involve regulations inside national borders.

Investment regulation, which has recently created such a firestorm on the multilateral level, is on the agenda. So are trade in services, government procurement practices, and intellectual property protection. Competition policy, which has not yet made it on to the agenda of the World Trade Organisation, will also be a part of the negotiations. The breadth of the negotiations will exceed even that of the Uruguay Round. The countries of the hemisphere have committed themselves to openness and transparency in the negotiating process. Toward that end, they have agreed to form a Committee on Civil Society to facilitate input from academia, labour and environmental groups, and the business community.

A timetable for the negotiations, along with the negotiation venues and a Chair and Vice-Chair for the comprehensive negotiations, has also been established (see Tables 8.3 and 8.4). The United States is pleased to have Canada chairing the negotiations during their initial phase, as well as to have that phase located in Miami. Canadian trade officials are highly sophisticated in the trade policy matters and should be able to get the negotiations off to a constructive start. Having the negotiations begin in Miami may help to build support for eventual fast-track authorisation in the United States Congress, particularly within the Florida delegation. Because the United States and Brazil are crucial players in

Table 8.3　Timetable, chairs and vice-chairs of the comprehensive negotiations

Dates	Chair	Vice-chair
1 May 1998–31 October 1999	Canada	Argentina
1 November 1999–30 April 2001	Argentina	Ecuador
1 May 2001–31 October 2002	Ecuador	Chile
1 November 2002–31 December 2004	Brazil and United States	Co-Chair

Table 8.4　Venues for the FTAA negotiations

1 May 1998–28 February 2001	Miami, United States
1 March 2001–28 February 2003	Panama City, Panama
1 March 2003–31 December 2004 (or until the end of the negotiations)	Mexico City, Mexico

the negotiations and have sometimes been at odds over the issues, they will co-chair the final phase of the negotiations.

While progress toward a Free Trade Area for the Americas has been delayed by the deadlock in the United States Congress, the process of regional economic integration in the hemisphere has by no means been arrested. Most Latin American countries have continued with economic reforms that are having a salutary economic effect for the region as a whole.

The Latin American economy grew by approximately 5.5 per cent in real terms during 1997, making possible a gain in real income per capita of 3.6 per cent.[8] Trade of Latin American countries is expanding twice as rapidly as overall world trade so that the region is regaining the share of world trade that it lost during the 1980s. Record amounts of private capital have flowed into the region as well. Net capital inflows amounted to 4 per cent of the region's Gross Domestic Product in 1997. Inflows of foreign direct investment into Latin America and the Caribbean increased by 52 per cent in 1996 alone, and the region accounted for almost one-third of all foreign direct investment into less developed countries.[9] By 1997, foreign direct investment in the region amounted to approximately 3.2 per cent of Gross Domestic Product, after having been less than 1 per cent of Gross Domestic Product throughout the 1979–93 period.

External debt as a percentage of Gross Domestic Product has also declined for the region. Disbursed external debt as a percentage of nominal Gross Domestic Product declined from greater than 50 per cent during the mid-1980s to around 33 per cent in 1997. This external debt is overwhelmingly long-term, with 62 per cent of it being private, as compared to 19 per cent shares for both bilateral and multilateral official debt. Foreign interest payments as a percentage of goods and services exports have declined, and have stabilised in the 12–13 per cent range.

A particularly dynamic part of the Latin American economy is MER-COSUR, the four-nation common market in the southern cone of South America. This subregional group includes the continent's two largest economies, Brazil and Argentina, along with Paraguay and Uruguay. Chile and Bolivia have recently become associate members of MERCO-SUR. The associate members of MERCOSUR have a combined population of 220 million people and a combined output of more than $1 trillion. Net foreign direct investment in the MERCOSUR countries increased by 33 per cent per year between 1990 and 1996, rising from $2.5 billion during this period to $18 billion.

Trade within MERCOSUR has more than quadrupled since 1990, and this group of countries has been the fastest growing part of the world economy, except for China, during the 1990s. Even so, the potential for further regional trade expansion is evident in the fact that intra-regional trade of the MERCOSUR countries accounts for only 2 per cent of the combined Gross Domestic Product of the member countries, as compared to $5\frac{1}{2}$ per cent for the NAFTA countries and 14 per cent for the European Union.[10]

Countries from outside the region have taken note of Latin America's changed economic prospects. The European Union, which is the largest trading partner of MERCOSUR, has entered discussions with MERCO-SUR, aiming toward a possible free trade agreement. Separate talks have also been scheduled between the European Union and the Andean Community countries. The European Union is the second largest trading partner of Mexico, and after more than three years of talks the European Union and Mexico have agreed negotiating guidelines with the intention of establishing a free trade accord by the year 2000 or 2001. Canada has signed a free trade agreement with Chile and has announced its intention to proceed with further agreements in Latin America. Japan also has expressed an interest in possible free trade agreements with Latin American countries.

The fact that other countries are moving more aggressively than the United States toward free trade agreements with Latin American countries is ironic. It was President George Bush's Enterprise for the Americas Initiative in 1990 which initially caught the imagination of Latin

American countries and kindled their interest in free trade agreements. A major goal of the Enterprise for the Americas Initiative was to encourage the economic reforms and democratisation which were underway in Latin America. That goal remained at least as valid and important at the end of the 1990s as it was at the beginning.

Effects of United States reticence toward hemispheric negotiations

The delay in being able to move ambitiously forward with the proposed Free Trade Area for the Americas is certainly embarrassing to the United States in its relations with its hemispheric neighbours. As mentioned earlier, the lack of fast-track authorisation also has adversely affected the ability of the United States to influence the agenda for the negotiations. Without a clear-cut mandate from the Congress to proceed with the negotiations, the United States Trade Representative has not been able to insist on including items of immediate and special interest to the United States.

Furthermore, the institutional structure of Western Hemispheric economic integration will evolve differently as a result of the delay. Had other countries in the hemisphere been able to accede to the NAFTA agreement, the institutions of NAFTA, which were still in their formative stages, would have been broadened to include the other countries. Because of the delay, not only will the NAFTA institutions have become established with only three member countries, but the institutions of MERCOSUR will have taken on a life of their own. A blending of the institutions of these two regional groups will be much more difficult than if Latin American countries had merely acceded to NAFTA. Fortunately, some of the sub-regional groupings that have been formed in Latin America are patterned after NAFTA, which will ease their eventual merger with NAFTA.

The uncertainty about the commitment of the United States to the Free Trade for the Americas negotiations may also be hindering further trade liberalisation measures by Latin American countries. These countries are naturally reluctant to eliminate restrictions that could be used as bargaining chips in eventual free trade negotiations with the United States. The pace of trade liberalisation in Latin America has undoubtedly slowed recently, partly as a result of the uncertainty surrounding the hemispheric trade negotiations, but also because the spillover effects of the Asian economic crisis and 'reform fatigue' have decreased enthusiasm for further globalisation and economic deregulation at this time.

The longer-term effects of United States reluctance to enter whole-heartedly into hemispheric negotiations, however, remain to be seen. Brazil would actually prefer to consolidate further its position within South America, perhaps through formation of a South American Free Trade Area, before engaging in serious negotiations for hemispheric free trade. Should this occur, as now seems likely, it could give the countries of Latin America a greater comfort level in their economic relations with the United States, an economy which is gigantic relative to most other Western Hemisphere economies. During 1997, when the United States president was denied fast-track authorisation for Free Trade Area for the Americas negotiations, public opinion polls throughout Latin America revealed an upsurge of support for a hemispheric free trade agreement. A somewhat reluctant United States is apparently viewed with less fear and suspicion in Latin America than would be the case if the United States were aggressively pursuing the free trade agenda.

Bringing Latin America into a free trade agreement with North America could make a great difference to the region's economic development prospects. Latin America is a region with tremendous potential, but also with several weaknesses. Some of the Latin American countries still labour under heavy debt burdens, and most have low savings rates. Transportation and communications infrastructures need to be modernised. The prices of both capital and labour frequently are distorted by ill-advised policies, and inflexible labour markets discourage job creation. The legal and other institutional framework of many countries is weak, so that property rights are not always adequately protected and law-enforcement is sometimes ineffective. Deficiencies in Latin American educational systems hinder the accumulation of human capital so important in a modern economy.[11]

The best hope for long-term economic development in Latin America is further deepening of the economic reform process that is well under-way in most countries. That is most likely to happen if the countries of Latin America are permitted to proceed with their anticipated free trade agreement with the United States. Increased interaction with the United States will strengthen the sometimes fragile democracies of the hemisphere, and will foster the macroeconomic stability essential for investors to make long-term commitments. Hemispheric cooperation and sharing of technical expertise will facilitate the modernisation of educational systems, the establishment of competent state bureaucracies, and improvement of judicial systems in the region. Hopes have been raised to a new level by the proposal for a Free Trade Area for the Americas, and the United States cannot back away from this proposal for an extended period of time without serious harm both to its relations with Latin America and to the economic outlook for the region.

Prospective trade agreements between Latin America and Western Europe may serve eventually to prod the United States Congress into action, and will be beneficial in their own right. However, the share of Europe in Latin America's trade has declined significantly during the past several years. Latin America's greatest potential for future trade expansion definitely lies within the Western Hemisphere.

Implications for transatlantic relations

Some observers have expressed concern that a Western Hemispheric free trade area might erect trade barriers to those outside the region. Others have worried that regionalism in the Western Hemisphere could drain away scarce bureaucratic resources of the foreign policy establishment in the United States, and divert attention from the World Trade Organisation or from important trading entities such as the European Union. Another concern is that trading relationships within the Western Hemisphere could be used as bargaining leverage against other areas such as Western Europe.[12]

Fortunately, there are good reasons to believe that none of these possible problems is likely to arise. The trade ministers of the Western Hemisphere have affirmed in each of the trade ministerial meetings that the Free Trade Area for the Americas must be fully compliant with World Trade Organisation obligations of the member countries. In the context of the rules-based international trading system that has evolved over the past fifty years, regional protectionism in the Western Hemisphere, or elsewhere, is unlikely. Periodic reviews by the World Trade Organisation hold the trading practices of both individual countries and regional trading groups up to international scrutiny. Greatly improved dispute settlement procedures in the World Trade Organisation now provide an effective mechanism for the redress of rules violations.

With regard to the possible diversion of United States attention from Europe to the Western Hemisphere, that, too, is highly improbable. The trading and investment relationships between the United States and Western Europe are so extensive and deep that they will command a major share of the attention of both regions. During the recent past the attention of the United States has focused considerably more often on Western Europe than on Latin America. The built-in agenda of the Uruguay Round has kept Western Europe and the United States heavily involved in trade talks concerning telecommunication services, information technology products and financial services. The Trans-Atlantic Business Dialogue has resulted in an agreement on mutual recognition of product standards and certification procedures which will facilitate transatlantic trade amounting to an estimated $40 billion. Trade disputes pertaining to property in Cuba, food safety issues, banana import regimes and aeroplane company mergers have kept the two regions focused on each other much of the time, and the intensity of their trade and investment relationships will mandate similar attention in the future.

In addition, plans for expansion of the North Atlantic Treaty Organisation have required much attention and close cooperation, as have a variety of other security issues. Geopolitical considerations will ensure that both the United States and Western Europe continue to devote a large share of their foreign policy resources to the transatlantic relationship.

As for expanded trading relationships within the Western Hemisphere possibly giving these countries increased leverage *vis-à-vis* entities such as the European Union, that should not be a major concern, at least for the near term. United States trade with all of Central and South America currently is only about one-third as great as United States trade with Western Europe, and the investment linkages are even more in Western Europe's favour. All things considered, the prospect of Western Hemispheric economic integration would seem to pose no threat whatsoever to the transatlantic relationship at this time.

Outlook for the future

The transatlantic trading relationship has grown robust on the foundation of strong cultural affinities, similarity of legal and political institutions, comparable levels of economic development, and shared values and goals in many areas. These common attributes have been, and will remain, powerful influences in the development of strong economic linkages across the Atlantic.

The geographical proximity of United States and Canada to Latin America do have an effect on their trade, and in some respects the Western Hemisphere comprises a natural trading area. However, differences in levels of economic development, cultural differences, wide disparities in economic size, and a history of strained relations have inhibited both formal and informal economic integration in the Western Hemisphere. While these differences are gradually being narrowed, they will remain significant impediments for some time to come.

The planned Free Trade Area for the Americas negotiations has no deadlines until the year 2005, except for a vague commitment that 'substantial progress' be made in the negotiations by the year 2000. Since the negotiations are to move forward only by consensus, progress is likely to be limited until the final deadline approaches. That being the case, the European Union conceivably could reach free trade agreements with Latin America before the United States does.[13] In that event, the 'transatlantic relationship' may be broadened to include Europe's relations with Latin America, just as the eastward expansion of NATO and the European Union are broadening the definition of transatlantic relations for the United States.

In March 1998 the European Union's External Relations Commissioner, Sir Leon Brittan, proposed to the member nations of the European Union a new transatlantic trade initiative to establish a Transatlantic Marketplace with the United States. That plan would have eliminated industrial tariffs by the year 2010 on a multilateral basis. The plan also provided for free trade in services on a preferential basis (with some exclusions), and further liberalisations in such areas as investment regulation, government procurement practices, and intellectual property protection. Even this ambitious plan, however, excluded the highly sensitive subjects of agriculture and audio-visual services. Nevertheless, the plan was not adopted because of reservations by certain European Union member states, particularly France.

At the Birmingham summit in May 1998 a document was issued outlining a Transatlantic Economic Partnership. This initiative appears to be a watered-down version of the Transatlantic Marketplace idea, although specifics of the plan were unclear at the time of this writing. The emphasis seems to be primarily on increased scientific cooperation and improved sharing of information to head off disputes relating to subjects such as food safety issues. With regard to services, the emphasis is on standardisation or harmonisation of future regulations as opposed to removing impediments already in place. Multilateral cooperation is anticipated in areas such as intellectual property protection, investment regulation and government procurement practices.

In addition to the proposed Free Trade Area for the Americas and the proposed Transatlantic Economic Partnership, countries along the Pacific Rim have, through the Asia-Pacific Economic Co-operation forum, made a commitment to work toward free trade among the developed countries by the year 2010, and among all of them by 2020. Given the number of countries involved in each of these initiatives and the share of world trade for which they collectively account, a strong case may be made for a new and comprehensive round of multilateral trade negotiations which would bring all of the other member countries of the World Trade Organisation into the negotiations. The built-in agenda of the Uruguay Round agreement requires that new multilateral talks on agriculture and services trade begin by the year 2000 in any case. Broadening the negotiations to a comprehensive round addressing all issues and including all of the member countries would further strengthen the world trading system. The essential catalyst for launching a new round of comprehensive negotiations is agreement between the United States and the European Union that such negotiations are desirable.

Notes

1 Nora Claudia Lustig, 'NAFTA: Setting the Record Straight', Brookings Policy Brief, No. 120, Brookings Institution, http://www.brook.edu/ES/POLICY/Polbrit20.html.

2 Richard Feinberg, 'Integrating the Americas', Trade Forum of the Americas, http://www.sice.oas.org/forum/non_govt/academic/Feinberg.htm.   Legislation considered under fast-track authorisation cannot be amended and must be either approved or rejected within 60 legislative days (90 days for revenue provisions such as import tariffs). Fast-track legislation was voted down for a second time in the United States House of Representatives on 25 September 1998.

3 'Between 1976 and 1990, total civilian employment grew by 33 percent in the United States (and by 19 percent in Japan) but by only 8 percent in Europe. And fully 97 percent of that increase was in the public sector.' Gregory Treverton, 'An Economic Agenda for the New Era', in David C. Gompert and F. Stephen Larrabee (eds), *America and Europe: a Partnership for a New Era* (Cambridge: Cambridge University Press, 1997), p. 58 (based upon OECD statistics).

4 For a survey of the empirical work, see J. David Richardson, 'Income Inequality and Trade: How to Think, What to Conclude', *Journal of Economic Perspectives*, vol. 9, no. 2, Spring 1995.

5 For a thorough examination of this issue, see Jagdish Bhagwati and Robert Hudec, *Fair Trade and Harmonization: Prerequisites for Free Trade?*, Vols I and II (Cambridge, Mass: MIT Press, 1996).

6 The relative cost advantage from less stringent environmental standards would tend to increase the exports of such a country and make its own import-competing goods more attractive, thus decreasing imports. The net effect would be to cause the country's currency to appreciate, offsetting the cost advantage from the lower environmental standards.

7 The 12 working groups were: Market Access; Customs Procedures and Rules of Origin; Investment; Standards and Technical Barriers to Trade; Sanitary and

Phytosanitary Measures; Subsidies, Antidumping and Countervailing Duties; Smaller Economies; Government Procurement; Intellectual Property Rights; Services; Competition Policy; and Dispute Settlement.

8 Economic growth in Latin America is expected to slow to, perhaps, 3.5 per cent during 1998 as a result of fallout in the region from the Asian economic crisis.

9 'World Direct Investment in 1996', *International Economic Review*, USITC Publication 3090, January/February 1998, pp. 27–30. Nevertheless, of United States direct investment abroad during 1993–96, all of Latin America accounted for 20.7 per cent, whereas Western Europe accounted for 52.6 per cent.

10 Carlos Sepulveda and Arturo Vera Aguirre, 'MERCOSUR: Achievements and Challenges', Inter-American Development Bank Working Paper Series 222, August 1997, p. 32. The trade infrastructure of the region is already being taxed by the recent trade growth, however, and is badly in need of expansion and modernisation. Unless this occurs, further trade expansion will be hindered.

11 Deficiencies in the educational systems of Latin America are widely recognised as a problem, and improvement of these systems was made a matter of high priority at the Second Summit of the Americas in 1998.

12 Miles Kahler, *Regional Futures and Transatlantic Economic Relations*, Council on Foreign Relations, 1995, pp. 22–5.

13 While a European Union–Latin American free trade agreement is conceivable, it does not seem likely. A major stumbling block would be the European Union stance on agriculture.

9
'Euroland vs Big Europe': EMU, Transatlantic Relations and the Eastern Enlargements of NATO and the European Union

Martin J. Dedman

Europe appears to be moving simultaneously in two different directions, with the European Union's (EU's) inward development of 'Euroland' and the outward growth of the EU and NATO into Big Europe. We are expected to believe that these two architectural frameworks for Europe in the twenty-first century will evolve together over the next few years and successfully coexist. Yet, Europe's two future institutional scenarios appear to have mutually incompatible objectives and deliver contradictory outcomes:

Euroland	Big Europe
11 states[a]	21 states[b]
Deeper	Wider
More integrated	Looser
Centralised	Less regulated
Weaker Transatlantic links	Stronger Transatlantic links
Euro rivals $	No single currency
Divisive	Non-divisive

[a] The current 15 EU states except for UK, Denmark, Sweden and Greece.
[b] The current 15 EU states plus Poland, Czech Republic, Hungary (i.e. NATO's expansion 1999) plus Estonia, Slovenia and Cyprus for the currently planned six-state EU enlargement [circa 2006?]. Any of the following might also be admitted to the EU if they are ready to join: Lithuania, Latvia, Romania, Bulgaria and Slovakia.

The original Maastricht conception of Euroland would inevitably mean a smaller, deeper, more integrated and centralised single currency zone requiring a rate of interest set by the European Central Bank, one monetary policy for the 11 states and ultimately one fiscal policy too. It would also be doubly divisive – within the EU itself between the ins and the outs (or 'pre-ins' as the EU Commission incongruously prefers!) and between the EU and the USA as the euro will rival the dollar.[1]

Big Europe, on the other hand, delivers a larger, looser, less regulated Europe, still very much based on the EU's Single European Market but with a radically overhauled Common Agricultural Policy (CAP) switching funds away from the system of price support (cutting guaranteed prices drastically and production subsidies for the biggest and most efficient farms) and towards direct aid payments. These plans for CAP form part of the EU's Agenda 2000 programme designed to prepare the EU for enlargement in Central and Eastern Europe in the first decade of the new century[2] – without them the CAP would be bankrupted.

Big Europe actually commenced when the 'New West' joined NATO in 1999 – this eastwards expansion to incorporate Poland, Hungary, and the Czech Republic is accompanied by closer western links between the EU and North America – an important component in a new European balancing act. The eastwards shift of NATO and its compensatory NATO–Russian Forum with a new working relationship between old Cold War adversaries is counterbalanced by the New Trans-Atlantic Agenda's closer cooperation between the EU and North America.[3] Its 'New Trans-Atlantic Market Place' also reduces the risk for the USA that it might be excluded, at some point in the future, from an enlarged EU's single market that it had nevertheless extended its Article 5 defence guarantee of nuclear protection to. In this way the USA avoids the trap that British Conservative administrations in the late 1950s fell into; namely defending the EEC through NATO while being excluded from its Common Market for 12 years (1961–73).[4]

The argument here is that Big Europe will develop but Euroland will not succeed (at least as envisaged at Maastricht and in the Treaty on European Union, 1992). The case here against Monetary Union (and so Euroland) succeeding is three-dimensional: a political component (that it is what EMU leads to, political federation, that rules it out); a historical dimension (that all non-commercial European integration has always failed and there is no reason to suppose it will succeed this time); and finally the economic argument (that Euroland is not an optimal currency area and so a single currency is unworkable).

Monetary Union and a single currency for the EU with the eventual disappearance of national currencies by mid-2002 simply will not happen because of what it would lead to – a Federal United States of Europe. Yet Euro-federalists insist that a federal Europe through the back door of Monetary Union is an inevitable and unstoppable process. Neofunctionalists too see moves towards a supranational superstate proceeding through successive 'spillovers'[5] – a common market in steel and coal (1951), leading to a general common market (1958), leading to a single market (1986), leading to a single currency (1999), and so to a European superstate and the end of the nation-states.

However, historical analysis of the process of European integration since it began in the late 1940s (in the Customs Union Study Group of 1948) and over the past 50 years shows that the Euro-federal inevitability thesis is a fantasy based on a misapprehension of history. Professor Alan Milward and others showed that Euro-federalism, far from being a driving force behind European integration, never had anything to do with it at all.[6] Moreover, historical research indicates that there are clear limits to the whole process of European integration: the only successful schemes have been economic or commercial, everything else having failed. Supranational schemes for military, political and atomic integration and monetary union in the past simply have not worked.[7] So why should they be expected to succeed in the future?

Only schemes for economic and commercial integration have worked because they were actually needed and wanted by the nation-states concerned (ECSC 1951, EEC 1958, SEA 1986). The motives and origin of these treaties were purely internal and essential to the nation-states concerned. The needs of postwar economic reconstruction and recovery were uppermost, and this required international cooperation. Milward argued that economic integration after 1945, far from leading to the eventual demise of the nation-state as neofunctionalists predict, actually 'rescued the nation state'.[8]

In contrast to this, the origination of those schemes of non-economic integration that failed was external to the nation-states themselves. For example, the initial impulse for the European Defence Community (EDC) scheme of 1950–54 came from outside: the outbreak of the Korean war and the consequent American demand for the swift rearmament of West Germany.[9]

Failed schemes tend to be ignored by political scientists as they do not fit their neofunctionalist model. For historians, a failure is as useful as a success in revealing the processes involved. The orthodox explanation for failure was that such attempts as the EDC were too ambitious and ahead of their time. However historical research suggests that the Pleven Plan in 1950, and the whole EDC episode, were in fact diplomatic devices for delay. They bought time, delayed German rearmament and NATO membership for five years and safeguarded the core bargain behind the Schuman Plan talks that started in June 1950, the very

month that the Korean war began. If West Germany had been able to
gain full sovereignty by putting 100 000 troops in NATO, as the US
wanted, it is doubtful that she would have made so many concessions
to France over access to German coal and the German steel market in the
Schuman Plan talks. The Pleven Plan safeguarded the Schuman Plan by
delaying German rearmament and so the restoration of German sovereignty by a route that would have been less beneficial to France.[10]

It appears, since 1945, that any German initiative or other event
threatening to alter West Germany's relationship with her neighbours
and her attachment to the West has consistently triggered one of three
stock reactions by France: developing closer links with Britain; pressing
for further European integration; or both together. So, for example, in
1969–70 West Germany had to conduct its Eastern policy (*Ostpolitik*) on
purely Soviet terms, following the Warsaw Pact's invasion of Czechoslovakia and the start of the Brezhnev Doctrine in 1968. This resurrected
fears in France of a new Rapallo Treaty (1922) – Germany seeking a
Russian *rapprochement* to achieve her objectives, in this case reunification
– or of West Germany becoming 'Finlandised'. This led directly to the
launch of the campaign for Economic and Monetary Union by 1980
(following the Werner Report of 1970) and also to closer ties with Britain
(reversing de Gaulle's policy and admitting the UK to the Common
Market).

In 1989–91, the collapse of Communism and the Soviet Empire, the
reunification of Germany and the eventual demise of the USSR itself
initially prompted President François Mitterrand to contemplate closer
ties with Britain, briefly but seriously, through an Anglo-French axis
inside the European Community. This was finally rejected, as it would
have jettisoned 40 years of successful French policy on Franco-German
relations. Instead, Mitterand and Kohl embarked on their rush to Maastricht and Monetary Union in the Treaty on European Union of February
1992. So events extraneous to the European Community tend to account
for the timing of initiatives for non-economic integration.[11]

Whatever else emerged from the past (or finally emerges from the
present) episode of EMU – a Monetary Union in the form of a single
currency was not and will not be one of them. What both episodes did
was to buy time, ten years in the case of the current effort (1992–2002),
and to keep Big Germany focused westwards on its relationship with
France, secured by France's old stock reaction.

However, one could say (wrongly as I will show) that these political
and historical arguments must be obsolete or fallacious as the euro
already exists. The pegged rates, irrevocably fixed on 1 January 1999,

were actually announced back in May 1998.[12] Yet, what is actually starting? The euro will exist purely as a unit of account with national currencies (pegged at the fixed rates) in circulation and with no euro notes and coins introduced until July 2001 at the earliest or July 2002 at the latest (by which time national currencies are supposed to be withdrawn). In fact, until 2002 there won't be a single currency but a twelfth one in effect.[13] It also means there exists (at least until July 2002) an option for reversal at no economic cost because national currencies are still in circulation. This leads us to the final economic argument against EMU succeeding – namely that it is unworkable.

The prevailing opinion among central bankers, numerous senior politicians and academics (including a letter calling for a postponement of the launch signed by 155 German economists)[14] is that EMU is now unstoppable but unsustainable as there are a number of intractable problems and serious blunders associated with the project.

There is no precedent for 11 nation-states having one currency, one interest rate, one central bank, one monetary policy and ultimately one fiscal policy. The International Gold Standard that prevailed between 1870 and 1914 is not comparable: commercial and fiscal policies were not common but national, and people were free to emigrate to the USA, Canada, South America and elsewhere – and millions did, an option no longer open today.

Euroland is also not an Optimal Currency Area partly because of the 'asymmetrical shock problem'. An extraneous shock might adversely affect one or two countries' economic prospects but not the rest. Yet there would be no national remedies available to solve the problem (the exchange rate and interest rate monetary tools have gone).[15] Under the Maastricht rules they cannot spend, they cannot borrow, they cannot alter interest rates and they cannot cut tax. Furthermore, there are no 'fiscal transfers' in Euroland, nor are there likely to be in the future, whereby tax revenues from one state can be spent on another in order to boost aggregate demand or reduce unemployment in a state in economic recession. The EU's budget is currently capped at just 1.27 per cent of the EU's GDP whereas the USA's federal budget, in what is an optimal currency area, amounts to 35 per cent of GDP. So in the EU there is no possibility of moving jobs to people via fiscal transfers.

In addition there is a lack of labour mobility and a lack of labour market flexibility in Euroland. In contrast to the USA (where, on average, US schoolchildren change school every three years because their parents move jobs), there is little interstate labour mobility in the EU. Language clearly is a significant barrier in Europe and one unlikely to decrease as the service sector continues to grow. So in the EU there is little possibility of moving people to jobs in other member states.[16]

The rigidity of the euro (as prescribed by the Maastricht rules) will force deregulation of labour markets (e.g. making it easier to hire and fire workers, increasing flexibility of wages, and lowering unemployment benefits), because if there is less monetary and fiscal flexibility there must be more labour market flexibility – which of course is attractive to big business in the EU. Meanwhile France and Italy have done the very opposite and reduced the working week to 35 hours. The French premier, Lionel Jospin, evidently believes the fallacy that if everyone works less, more people can work, proving that for every difficult problem there is a simple wrong answer, as the volume of labour demand is not fixed in an economy. In fact the very reverse is true: where there are longer working hours per employee there is less unemployment.

The great paradox of Monetary Union was always that it was bound to deliver a healthy dose of supply-side reforms and Anglo-Saxon neo-classical economics to Continental corporatism – i.e. more Hayek, less Keynes. Yet, despite the Delors White Paper of 1993, outlining the need for a flexible labour market in the EU, there have been few signs of any national acceptance let alone compliance with this.

Since the SPD's 1998 election victory in Germany there has been much talk of a 'red euro' that should prioritise unemployment as the principal enemy, rather than inflation. There have also been reports of intentions to redraw and relax the Maastricht rules and Stability Pact to permit greater fiscal flexibility (governments being allowed to exceed the 3 per cent GDP spending limit when the excess is for investment).[17] Such fiscal flexibility is presumably intended to avoid implementing the much-needed flexible labour market reforms in Euroland by ensuring that the euro is weak. This should boost net exports and therefore employment, all by undermining international confidence in the euro.

It is also clear that there is a basic lack of economic convergence between the 11 states of Euroland. The Maastricht criteria (though seem-ingly observed as much in the breach as in compliance) focused on monetary and fiscal targets rather than indices like unemployment rates. These vary enormously in Euroland with 21 per cent in Spain, 9.7 per cent in Germany, 12.5 per cent in France and 5.5 per cent in the Netherlands.[18] Is it really sustainable to have one interest rate in these circumstances without fiscal transfers?

There is also the problem of debt and in particular what has been called the 'explosive debt dynamics of unfunded state pensions' in Ger-many, France and Italy – posing a future actuarial crisis due to their demographics and funding of pensions from general tax revenue.[19] Fiscal integration in Euroland might ultimately result in more prudent member states contributing towards other countries' state pensions. Euroland could also mean that national public debt is eventually pooled – much to the advantage of Italy (with a debt at 122 per cent of GDP) and Belgium (national debt at 127 per cent of GDP), a prospect that is unlikely to encourage future debt reduction by those states.

The 'excess deficits procedure' always looked a weak contrivance since it was devised (at Chancellor Kohl's insistence in 1996–97) to enforce fiscal rigour in Euroland, with discipline supposedly maintained when necessary by fining transgressor member states. The Stability Pact operates through qualified majority voting, which means one state in breach of the pact might be vulnerable to sanctions; but what if several members breached the pact (coincidentally or in concert)? Could the pact be enforced and excess deficits prevented?

Since Chancellor Kohl and the CDU lost the election in September 1998, the Stability Pact and the euro look considerably weaker as a result of the apparent SPD strategy of having a soft euro from the start, leading the other Euroland governments in a push for greater political control of the euro[20] and for higher government spending to counter the economic downturn. These are policies that at face-value represent a horrific prospect for the ECB and the German banking community, and they jeopardise the wealth of the German people.

It used to be considered erroneous to think that the EMU and its predecessor the ERM could ever be operated in the 'community interest' or in the interest of the European Union as a whole. After all what was this Union interest? There was seemingly no such thing, as Bernard Connolly's whistleblowing book revealed.[21] In any case, for years the views of France and Germany over euro policy and the ECB fundamentally diverged. Throughout the Kohl–Mitterrand and Kohl–Chirac eras (despite displays of harmony periodically by holding hands at war memorials) the French always wanted a soft euro, the Germans a hard one and the French and German electorates were being promised different things by their leaders.[22] If the euro were run on German lines, France would be in trouble as it had always refused to be in a Deutschmark zone. It was also assumed that if the euro were run the French way, the Germans would wreck it. Now however, Chancellor Gerhard Schröder and his Finance Ministers have either decided to shake international confidence in the euro and so undermine the whole project or the Germans have resolved their seemingly irreconcilable conflict over the strength of the euro and opted for the soft French model.

Whichever the case, the euro scheme has a built-in design fault: the way it has been set up and timetabled means that it contains a one-way bet blunder.[23] Speculators have nothing to lose in exchanging Lira for D-marks at the fixed rate, waiting for the scheme's collapse (and so for fixed rates to unstick) when the D-mark will appreciate and the Lira fall (offering all speculators the opportunity for profit by converting back). George Soros made a similar one-way bet on sterling's exit from the Exchange Rate Mechanism in 1992. His Berkshire Fund currently contains a cash mountain of $9 billion. Such speculative turmoil would be very damaging, particularly to German export industries.

Overall, the economic prospects and feasibility of the planned single currency look bleak; historical analysis indicates that there have always been limits to and mixed motives for European integration schemes, a fact that is often overlooked.[24] Furthermore, Monetary Union will put the Single European Market at risk unless Political Union occurs first or soon after. There is no popular support for a United States of Europe and no mandate for it, the tide of history having moved on and against federalist solutions and systems (viz. the demise, often bloody, of Yugoslavia and the USSR).

An eventual collapse of Monetary Union and the whole Single Currency Plan has potentially huge repercussions and might put the whole EU at risk. One obvious solution would be to retain the euro as a common currency – i.e. a parallel currency – circulating alongside national currencies, which *de facto* it is anyway until 2002. This would not require Monetary Union and it avoids the Euroland scenario outlined at the start of this chapter. Also, the use of a common currency would reduce big business's transaction costs within the EU just as a single currency would. On the other hand, a parallel currency would mean higher menu costs because of dual pricing, and Gresham's Law would operate whereby bad currency drives out good currency as the means of exchange. Incidentally, what is 'bad' would vary from country to country depending on the exchange rate between each country's currency and the euro.

Another advantage of a common currency is that it would not prove as divisive as the single currency. The UK, for one, would be less likely to object to it. In fact one of Margaret Thatcher's Chancellors of the Exchequer, Nigel Lawson, proposed just such a thing ('the hard ecu' plan) a decade ago.

In contrast to Euroland's Monetary Union, which would require a political federation resulting in the effective demise of the nation-state, the start of 'Big Europe' with NATO's Eastern enlargement would do the very opposite because NATO is about *preserving* nation-states. Also, whereas Euroland is a particularly French answer to the German Question, Big Europe partly answers both the German and Russian Questions and to the satisfaction of several more states. The emerging complete solution to the post-Cold War German and Russian Questions has four components: the creation of Big Europe through the Eastern enlargement of NATO (1999) and the proposed Eastern enlargement of the EU, the New Trans-Atlantic Agenda (1995) and the Founding Act (1997).

In addition, one could also add the development of the G7 into a G8.[25] Admitting Russia to some G7 meetings was in fact partly a reward for Russian acquiescence in the intended NATO enlargement – described as 'Western psychotherapy' for Russia by a Moscow official, and another source of future photo-opportunities for Boris Yeltsin as a Russian president involved in global decision-making.

The foreign policy initiative for Eastern enlargement now lies in NATO's hands rather than the EU's. Both Douglas Hurd and Malcolm Rifkind, the last two Conservative Foreign Secretaries, considered the Common Foreign and Security Policy (CFSP) of the EU to be never more than 70 per cent effective (unlike NATO). The USA always preferred simultaneous EU/NATO enlargement partly because of the threat of the Western European Union (WEU) becoming the EU's separate defence arm. This might result in states joining the EU and the WEU but not NATO. They would then be under US protection but not US influence.[26] However this is now less of a threat as the UK, Denmark and Ireland continue to oppose the WEU being the EU's defence arm and, following the 1995 Alpine–Nordic enlargement, three more neutral states can be relied on to oppose it.

There are several obvious geopolitical reasons for expanding NATO eastwards, the first being the need to fill the security vacuum and the need for stability in the East. Also, if there is no enlargement to the East, is the West saying that Central and Eastern Europe is permanently expendable or that the EU is only a 'rich man's club'? In 1938, 1939, 1945, 1947, 1956 and 1968, the West was powerless to do anything much for Central and Eastern Europe. The situation now is different. Does the West still do nothing? Germany is keen to stop being the 'last country in the West', the most easterly member of NATO. Poland is less than 40 miles from Berlin, the German government's new capital. Germany too feels more secure if Poland is in NATO. Germans, it is said, harbour submerged fears of 'dangers from the East' because of what happened to female civilians in 1945. Enlargement also dulls Germany's temptation to adopt wayward policies towards Russia, as in 1914 and 1941. So Russia and other states should be reassured.[27] In fact, there is something for everyone, even Russia, in NATO's Eastern enlargement – except for those left out.

NATO enlargement has been criticised though, particularly by two heavyweights, George Kennan and Henry Kissinger, who respectively described it as being 'a grave error' and the 'biggest post war error'. The danger they saw was that NATO's enlargement to the East might inflame Russian nationalism and increase the risk of militarism there. It has also been attacked on the grounds of cost. However, the cost need not be that great. The 'NATO-Lite' option could mean modest weapon upgrades, estimated at £1.2 billion over ten years, to make forces interoperable. Enlargement will result in dilution though, as the NATO–Russian Forum (Founding Act 1997) dilutes NATO's Council, mission and psychological resolve. NATO's oft-stated mantra of 'no plan, no reason, no intent', intended to reassure Russia, does not strengthen deterrence. Henry Kissinger remembers too that 'condominium' (détente between the US and USSR) in the 1970s weakened NATO.[28]

Hopefully, such critical assessments will prove overly pessimistic. Deterrence, after all, needs only to be proportionate to the threat. Also, NATO is really *for* something: it does not need a 'bad object' to be against in order to survive and flourish. When facts change, as in 1989–91, ideas invariably have to. NATO's reaction to the Balkan crisis in indicative.

The motives behind the EU's enlargement eastwards are, like NATO's, partly political. EU membership is an opportunity to consolidate stability in Central and Eastern Europe (CEE) and also a reward for ending authoritarianism and an incentive to guarantee the confirmation of democracy and the market economy (this also applied to Greece, Spain and Portugal in the 1970s when they ended military governments). Eastern enlargement of the EU will increase the EU's political weight in the world (e.g. in WTO negotiations). A similar phenomenon occurred when Spain and Portugal joined the EC in 1986 with the result that the EU's relations with Latin America improved considerably. Of course, enlargement would shift the balance in the EU eastwards. Ireland, Greece and Luxembourg fear this because, as small states, their influence and benefits (in the case of the first two) would inevitably shrink.

Germany and Britain are both keen on enlargement eastwards. In the UK's case, this is probably because a bigger EU might well result in a looser organisation (perhaps restricted to just a Single European Market), and it also means that major reforms to the Common Agricultural Policy would be an essential precondition. For CEE of course, membership of both the EU and NATO is a chance to build themselves into the West and away from Russia.

Economic factors are also crucial in the EU's eastern enlargement. EU exports to CEE increased 185 per cent during 1989–94 (their value trebled), whereas EU imports from CEE increased 130 per cent in the same period. The EU enjoys a big trade surplus with the CEE.[29]

In 1996, Germany accounted for 52 per cent of the EU's total trade with CEE while France accounted for 8 per cent and the UK 6 per cent. Germany also accounted for 23 per cent of Foreign Direct Investment (FDI) in CEE, France for 6 per cent, the US 14 per cent and Austria 14 per cent.[30] Germany therefore has a massively disproportionate economic influence in CEE and German commercial power and leverage will increase with enlargement. Two-thirds of all German speakers outside Germany live in CEE. The trade and cultural ties with Germany have been strong for centuries. Germany has been both an inspirational model and a painful experience for CEE this century.

Germany today is the world's third biggest economy. German GDP is roughly equal to French and UK GDP combined. In contrast, the Russian economy is roughly the size of Belgium's or Greater London's (Russian GDP has fallen 40 per cent since 1993, following the loss of two empires in just three years). Russia, with 148 million people, receives only a third of the FDI that Hungary, with 11 million people, attracts. Germany is a veritable economic colossus (despite its current economic problems). Russia is an economic midget in comparison. Germany has 22 per cent of the EU's population, accounts for 30 per cent of EU GDP and provides 30 per cent of EU revenue.

The 'new *Ostpolitik*' of CEE enlargement can only increase German economic and political influence and so enhance its diplomatic weight generally. Hence the attraction and need for a counterbalance to Eastern enlargement in the form of closer EU–North American ties.

Twenty-five years ago, UK entry to the EEC, agreed in principle in 1969 and a reality from 1973, was the counterweight to West Germany's *Ostpolitik* of 1968–72 (conducted on Soviet terms following the invasion of Czechoslovakia). However, we must first consider two very big problems concerning the EU's enlargement to the East: the potential cost under the EU's existing common policies (agriculture and regional funds), and the constitutional reforms needed for the EU to enlarge from 15 to 21 and eventually 26 states.[31]

Absorbing large poor agricultural states like Poland has always been difficult for the EU (and its forerunners, the EEC and EC). This was the case with Spain in 1986 and the reason why negotiations were so protracted and difficult, taking eight years, from 1978 to 1986. Such poor new entrants are a big expense because they are big net recipients from the EU's budget, whereas small, rich, industrialised states are easily absorbed as future net contributors to EU coffers. The Alpine–Nordic enlargement of 1995, for example, took the EU from 12 to 15 states with the addition of Finland, Sweden and Austria, three new entrants able to help bankroll EU enlargement to the East.

Estimates suggest that the EU's budget could increase by between 30 and 50 per cent if CEE states joined under current policies. Poland alone has 35 million people including 8.5 million farmers (smallholders who were never collectivised). Polish agriculture has more in common with seventeenth-century English husbandry with its horses, crop rotation and fields lying fallow than with twentieth-century farming practice. Nevertheless, Poland grows as much wheat as France and as many potatoes as the whole of the EU!

The budgetary implications of bringing Poland into the existing CAP regime and Poland's need for structural assistance from the Regional Development Fund represents the major financial obstacle to EU enlargement. CAP reform is therefore an essential prerequisite for CEE enlargement.[32] However the big difficulty with reforming CAP is not in devising suitable macro-economic solutions, but the absence of sufficient political will in many states to endorse reform. Chancellor Kohl and his CDU in Germany, for example, were dependent on 600 000 German farming family votes to be re-elected (he didn't get enough of them). Consequently little at all was proposed let alone done to the CAP before the German elections in September 1998.

Another necessary precondition for EU enlargement beyond the current 15 members is much-needed constitutional reform of the EU's decision-making process, as well as changes to the powers and privileges of existing member states. Without such changes, decision-making will be gridlocked and the EU will effectively grind to a halt. However, despite the EU's Intergovernmental Conference of 1996–97 on constitutional change and Treaty revision, the Amsterdam summit of EU heads of state in June 1997 avoided hard decisions and postponed any constitutional reform. The scene had hardly changed by the summer summit of 1999. Existing small members, in particular, clung to their privileged constitutional position, enshrined originally in the Treaties of Paris (1951) and Rome (1957), giving them, for example, disproportionate voting power in the Council of Ministers and over-representation in the European Parliament. All of this and much else will need to change prior to EU enlargement.

NATO's enlargement proved simpler and easier to facilitate than the EU's. Consequently, we are unlikely to see Big Europe grow through the simultaneous expansion of the EU and NATO but rather through enlargement in tandem: NATO's first, followed by the EU's.[33] The only available counterbalance to the 'New *Ostpolitik*' of the 1990s is a much closer relationship with North America. The New Trans-Atlantic Agenda (NTAA) signed in December 1995 at the EU–US Madrid summit is (with a similar agreement between the EU and Canada, signed in February 1996)[34] the counterweight to Eastern enlargement and growing German influence in CEE and inside the EU. For America, it also represents the *quid pro quo* for extending America's protection and nuclear umbrella to the East and reassuring the US that she will not be excluded commercially from a possible 'Fortress Europe', a future 22-state EU that continued to rely on US security guarantees. The NTAA is more an expression of mutual aspirations, shared beliefs and statements of intent rather than a treaty with a series of specific commitments. It refers to the creation of a 'New Trans-Atlantic Marketplace', with the elimination of tariffs, non-tariff barriers and the resolution of EU–US disputes (over such things as the Boeing-McDonnell Douglas Merger, the Helms-Burton/Cuban trade issue, bananas or hormone-fed beef); and establishment of a 'Trans-Atlantic Economic Space' between NAFTA and the EU's Single European Market, with the key objectives of mutual recognition and common standards on EU and US products.[35] The current European Commission proposal to liberalise EU–US trade might be worth 150 billion ecu p.a. (£99 billion) to Europe after the first five years. Two-way trade in goods and services amounted to 355 billion ecu in 1996 with the EU and US already accounting for 19 per cent of each other's trade in goods.

'Building more bridges' across the Atlantic through the NTAA is not simply a commercial matter. It also incorporates provision for joint EU–US responses to global threats such as those from drugs and terrorism and specifically refers to the joint promotion of peace, stability, democracy and development 'especially in Eastern Europe'. A revitalised and closer transatlantic partnership, particularly between North America's NAFTA and the EU's SEM essentially complements and balances Eastern enlargement and is an integral part of the whole process.[36]

Whatever happens to Euroland between 1999 and 2002, Big Europe's commercial, military and political future is not dependent on Monetary Union but on the Agenda 2000 proposals, the European Conference process, NATO's enlargement, the NATO–Russian Council and the NTAA, particularly its New Trans-Atlantic Marketplace. It is no coincidence that these separate threads are being wound together at the same time to securely unite more states than ever before.

On the other hand, official and unofficial EU resistance to imports from US distributors and exporters, often in the face of findings in favour of the US by the World Trade Organisation, to which both belong, raises serious doubts as to whether those in control of EU policy will not sabotage the Atlantic counterweight that eases Eastward expansion and, with it, the American sheet anchor that secures European stability.

Notes

1   See Anne Segall, 'Everything to play for against the Dollar', *Daily Telegraph*, 2 May 1998.
2   The inaugural 'European Conference' was held in March 1998 at Lancaster House, London, to formally launch what will be a long process of preparation by the EU and prospective members to make the financial and constitutional reforms for 2000–2006.
3   EU Press Release 122, 96/95 on Joint EU–US Action Plan for deepening and expanding EU–US relations.
4   M.J. Dedman, *The Origins and Development of the European Union 1945–95* (London: Routledge, 1996), pp. 93–4.
5   Ibid., p. 9.
6   A.S. Milward, *The European Rescue of the Nation State* (London: Routledge, 1992), pp. 14–18; *The Frontier of National Sovereignty: History and Theory 1945–92* (London: Routledge, 1993), pp. 3–5.
7   M.J. Dedman, 'The Atlantic Alliance, the European Union and an "Ever Closer Union"?' in Douglas Eden (ed.), *The Future of the Atlantic Community* (London: Middlesex University Press, 1997), pp. 105–7.
8   Milward (1992), pp. 18–28.
9   Dedman (1996), Chap. 5, 'German rearmament, the European Defence Community and the demise of the European Army, 1950–54'.
10 M.J. Dedman, 'European Integration: Origins and Motives', *Modern History Review*, vol. 9, no. 2, November 1997, p. 33.
11 M.J. Dedman in Eden (1997), pp. 112–13.
12 See *Financial Times*, 2 May 1998. The euro is equivalent to, for example, 1.977 German DM; 6.630 French francs; 1952 Italian lira.
13 Professor Tim Congdon (MD of Lombard St Research), writing in the *Daily Telegraph*, 10 February 1998.
14 See Eddie George's comments in *Time* and *Independent*, 30 January 1998; *Daily Telegraph*, 30 March 1998. Also, Alan Greenspan's comments quoted from the *Wall Street Journal*; *Guardian*, 13 February 1998, 'UNICE – Europe's Employers Federations warning of the lack of preparedness for Euro'; *Financial Times*, 10 February 1998, '155 German economists call for a two-year "orderly post-ponement" '.

15 See Larry Elliott (*Guardian* Economics Editor), writing in *Sunday Times*, 12 July 1998.
16 Ibid.
17 'Battle for control of Euro-Bank' in *The Times*, 17 November 1998.
18 ILO's Standardised Unemployment Rates, *Eurostats*, March 1997.
19 Germany, France and Italy each have a pension debt of more than 100 per cent of GDP; the UK's is less than 20 per cent of GDP.
20 *Financial Times*, 27 September 1998; *Guardian*, 27 October 1998.
21 Bernard Connolly, *The Rotten Heart of Europe: the Dirty War for Europe's Money* (London: Faber & Faber, 1995). The author was the senior Commission official responsible for EMS affairs.
22 Ibid., p. 391.
23 See C. Lockwood in the *Daily Telegraph*, 8 September 1997.
24 M.J. Dedman, 'EMU the first time around', in *History Today* 48, 1, January 1998, pp. 5–7.
25 *Daily Telegraph*, 19 June 1997, p. 8; and 28 May 1997, pp. 1–2.
26 G. Heather and H. Kirsty, *Eastward Enlargement of the European Union* (London: Chatham House, 1997); J. Gower, *Crisis or Opportunity? Enlargement to Central and Eastern Europe* (London: Centre for European Studies, 1996).
27 *Sunday Times*, 18 May 1997, p. 18.
28 *Sunday Times*, 16 February 1997, p. 16 and 18 May 1997, p. 18; *Daily Telegraph*, 10 July 1997, p. 24, and 11 April 1997, p. 18.
29 *Eurostats*, 1997; J. Cook, 'A survey on Germany', *Business in Central Europe*, December 1996.
30 K. Lowry and J. Templeman, 'Germany's New Eastern Bloc', *Business Week*, 3 February 1997.
31 *Sunday Times*, 15 July 1997.
32 See C. Southey, 'Seeking an agricultural policy for a wider EU', *Financial Times*, 16 January 1995; and 'No farm reform, no EU enlargement', *Financial Times*, 24 November 1995.
33 NATO's fiftieth anniversary in 1999 saw the admission of Poland, the Czech Republic and Hungary to membership, whereas the EU's fifth enlargement, with up to six new states, will not take place before 2005 and perhaps later.
34 Council of EU, General Secretariat Press Release 122 96/95 (Presse 35 6 G) on EU–US Summit, 3 December 1995, and Joint Action Plan for New Trans-Atlantic Agenda; EU–Canada New Agreement, 18 December 1996 (1P/96/1176) Joint Political Declaration and EU–Canada Action Plan adopted at Ottawa Summit.
35 EU Press Release 122 96/95 on Joint EU–US Action Plan for deepening and expanding EU–US relations as a framework with four shared goals, pp. 12–39.
36 See Summary of Report, 'Perspective on Trans-Atlantic Relations,' November 1995, produced by Forward Studies Unit of the EU, Brookings Institute, Washington, and the Stiftung für Wissenschaft und Politik, Eberhausen. This is the background study that reviewed US–EU relations and reveals the thinking behind the NTAA. Regular EU–US summits can clear the air on disputed issues – e.g. policy on Cuba and Chinese accession to the WTO (EU Press Release WE/45/96 19 December 1996). The NTAA is a very wide-ranging programme of cooperation between the EU and the US and Canada.

10
The Transatlantic Implications of European Monetary Union

Martin Holmes

Introduction

There are, I believe, five major implications of monetary union for the transatlantic relationship, all of them damaging, and all of them will retard genuine cooperation between Europe and the North American continent; but before I come to those five points in detail, it is necessary to make some important introductory points.

Firstly let me say that I am a strong supporter of the transatlantic relationship and an unequivocal supporter of NATO, believing in co-operation between Europe and North America. However, I am not a supporter of the process of internal political and economic integration within the European Union. I believe that Europe should remain a continent; it should not seek to become a country, with its own flag, its own anthem, its own currency, and its own political system, leading to a centralised federal political entity. My own position is very similar to that espoused by former Prime Minister Margaret Thatcher in the 1988 Bruges speech when she argued in favour of European cooperation and free trade between nation states, but opposed any centralised superstate. Of course there are many people who would prefer a Europe of nation-states but tolerate the current process of integration. This is the policy of the present government as it was of John Major's government. This is not my view. I am positively opposed to the current process of integration in Europe both for political reasons, because I think it is undemocratic, and for economic reasons, because I am a globalist, not a European region-alist. Free trade on a global basis is preferable to a European customs union.

Let me admit at once that this is a minority view on both sides of the Atlantic. It has always been the case that American administrations from

Harry Truman's onwards have supported European integration largely because during the Cold War the United States wanted to bolster the interests of the Western World and NATO by encouraging European cooperation. Moreover many Americans thought that the process of European integration would be similar to the process of the integration of the United States itself. Just as 50 states have been admitted to the Union and free market economics has come to dominate in the United States, so European integration would create a replica of the United States in Europe, leading ultimately to a United States of Europe, which would be a trading partner cooperating with the United States in a true Atlantic partnership.

Central to this process was the way in which the American administrations wanted to create a quite different Germany from that of the *Hitlerzeit* by encouraging a democratic federal West Germany committed to the western alliance. Truman's Secretary of State, Dean Acheson, in his memoirs, *Present at the Creation*, wrote of his meeting with Konrad Adenauer,

> His great concern was to integrate Germany completely into Western Europe. Indeed, he gave this end priority over the reunification of unhappily divided Germany, and could see why her neighbours might look upon it as almost a precondition to reunification. He wanted Germans to be citizens of Europe, to cooperate, with France especially, in developing common interests and outlook and in burying the rivalries of the past few centuries. Their common heritage had come to them down the Rhine, as the successors of Charlemagne, who guarded European civilisation when human sacrifice was still practised in eastern Germany. They must lead in the rebirth of Europe.[1]

The Americans also encouraged British governments to join the process. When the Churchill and Eden government decided that they would support European integration but not partake of it, the American administration made clear its opposition. The Americans later encouraged the Macmillan, Wilson and Heath governments to join the EEC. During 1974–75, when there was the prospect during the renegotiation of the terms of entry by the Wilson government, that Britain might be expelled from the European community or might withdraw, Henry Kissinger personally intervened to dissuade Jim Callaghan, the Foreign Secretary, from contemplating this option.

The United States hoped that, when the British joined, they would make the European community Atlanticist. The Americans believed that the British could lead, shape, mould and change Europe, a view which was, even then, over-optimistic, and exaggerated any capacity of changing what was essentially a Franco-German enterprise.

It is now more widely understood that the single European currency is part of a political project which began in the 1950s with the Treaty of Rome and which reached maturity with the Maastricht Treaty which was ratified in 1993. From the start political will has fuelled the creation of a political and federal superstate, in which the continental countries and the founding fathers of Europe intended integration to intertwine political and economic integration. As Helmut Kohl has admitted on the relationship of the single currency to political union, 'we want the political unification of Europe. If there is no monetary union there cannot be political union and vice versa. A European police force and army lie at the end of the road to political union'. Monetary union is inconsistent with British sovereignty and self-government which is why virtually all Eurosceptics are opposed to it on principle. What remains surprising is that some British supporters of Economic and Monetary Union (EMU) downplay, or ignore, its political dimension by citing only reduced transaction costs and the avoidance of exchange rate risk.

1970s external shocks

Another reason why the continentals are so determined to go ahead with the single currency is because they want the current plan to avoid the fate of its 1970s predecessor, the Werner Report. Werner envisaged European monetary union by 1980 and many of the features of that 1970 plan were later incorporated into the 1989 Delors Report. Werner envisaged European Community currencies being freely convertible; the parities being irrevocably fixed; community currencies being replaced by one single currency; the centralisation of monetary and credit policy; a unified policy on capital markets; a centralised budgetary policy; institutional changes to influence national budgets and a Community central banking system. Delors reinvented the Exchange Rate Mechanism (ERM) as the instrument for achieving monetary union, and the convergence criteria were added by the Maastricht Treaty. Essentially the 1990s plan is a 'microwaved' version of the 1970s plan.

But external shocks meant that Werner proved abortive. Firstly there was the collapse of the Bretton Woods system of the fixed exchange rates; secondly there was the oil price crisis of 1973–74 when the price of oil quadrupled; and thirdly the British renegotiation of the terms of EEC entry by the Wilson government completely dominated the diplomatic agenda up to the 1975 referendum. Those three factors together meant that it was not possible to complete the project by 1980 because European leaders lacked the necessary political will. The current generation of European federalists consequently are absolutely determined that this time no external shocks will derail the project, despite the fact that the 1990s external shocks have been of a similar magnitude to those which proved fatal in the 1970s.

1990s external shocks

Firstly, the Danes voted in June 1992 to reject the Maastricht Treaty lock, stock and barrel. That democratic judgement invalidated the treaty even according to the legal requirements of the treaty itself, but the European elite, ignoring that fact, made the Danes vote again in a disgraceful contempt of democracy. Secondly, during 1992 and 1993 the exchange rate mechanism, which was the device to bring about a single European currency, imploded. The narrow ($2\frac{1}{4}$ per cent) and wide (6 per cent) bands were abandoned and extended to a 15 per cent band as a result of the finance ministers' meeting of 2 August 1993. It may be argued that this invalidated the whole project of monetary union which was based on the inviolability of the narrow bands. But the European elite ignored that external shock. Thirdly, as the March 1998 EMI report conceded, with the exception of Luxembourg, none of the other participating countries have met the convergence criteria which the Maastricht Treaty itself laid out. A whole series of smoke-and-mirrors technical adjustments have occurred in country after country. The Italian special 'Euro-tax', the French fiddle with the telecom pension arrangements, the Belgian attempt to completely redesign how their public sector deficit is construed, and the Irish attempt to claim that money they received for agricultural subsidies and cohesion funds is a product of their own economy rather than handed out by net EU budget contributors, have enabled the convergence criteria to be ignored.

The evidence from the 1990s is that the European elite is absolutely determined to procure the single currency. Being guided by political will, and fearful of what happened last time, nothing is going to stop them. As former Chancellor and Maastricht negotiator Norman Lamont has argued:

> How can anyone believe in the impartial rule of law in the EU any longer? Treaties are meaningless and ignored when they are inconvenient. Politics drives all. When we negotiated the convergence

criteria at Maastricht in 1992 we meant them to be observed and not to be fudged in this way. It is quite clear that the convergence criteria laid down at Maastricht have been seriously breached by several countries: Article 104c and Protocol 5 of the Maastricht Treaty indicate that qualifying countries must have a debt to GDP ratio of less than 60% 'unless the ratio is sufficiently diminishing and approaching the reference value'. Since Maastricht was signed Germany's debt to GDP ratio has increased from 44.1% to 61.2%, Austria's from 58% to 68.9%, Spain's from 48.3% to 69.8%, Portugal's from 60.7% to 62.4% and Italy's from 108.7% to 122%. Belgium's has fallen by over 5 percentage points but remains at 123.6 twice the level specified in Maastricht. How can a tax like Italy's Eurotax, to be levied in 1997 and to be repaid in 1999 up to 70%, be described as a 'lasting reduction in the fiscal deficit'?[2]

One possible future external shock has been raised by Dr Walter Eltis, who argued in a paper published by the Centre for Policy Studies (CPS) in 1997 that, between 1999 when stage 3 of the project begins and 2002 when the single currency replaces the European currencies, international currency dealers still have the opportunity to wreck the whole project. Dr Eltis argues that what happened to the ERM in 1992–93 might happen in the three-year intervening period. As Dr Eltis puts it:

It is beginning to be understood that its creators perpetrated an incredible blunder by leaving [the euro] wide open to international speculation for 36 months between the start date of 1 January 1999, when all the participating currencies will remain legal tender, and 31 December 2001 when they will finally be superseded by the euro. A collapse during the three years in which national currencies will remain legal tender would create an opening for banks and hedge funds to profit hugely at the expense of the participating government as in 1992. Some of Europe's governments will have an inescapable obligation to defend with all the resources at their disposal the exchange rate structure agreed at the end of 1998, while George Soros and others who command international financial resources will be free to express a costless preference for the Deutsche mark or the guilder over the lira, the peseta or the franc. A breakdown in agreed exchange rates cannot possibly result in a raise in their value against the mark. But if there is any breach in the EMU dike, hedge funds will again make billions from the resulting fall of the lira, the peseta, the French franc or indeed the Belgian franc. The creators of

EMU have astonishingly agreed to allow the world's financial community three complete years of a costless one way option'.[3]

It is certainly possible there will be another external shock resulting from foreign exchange turbulence; but even if that occurs, the European elite will still carry on with the project. One prominent supporter of EMU, Professor Richard Portes, may thus be correct to argue that the EU would treat any asymmetric shock as a 'debt crisis' rather than a 'currency crisis'. In response to Dr Eltis' supposition Professor Portes retorts that:

This will not be a fixed exchange rate system, and hence not subject to speculative attack. If holders of Italian lire (say) want D-marks instead, the Bundesbank will be willing to purchase as much as the entire Italian money supply at the fixed accounting rate. It would accumulate claims denominated in euros, with an explicit 'exchange-rate guarantee' from governments. Not to honour the guarantee would be to abrogate the Maastricht Treaty, with huge political costs – not an option for a central bank. And the monetary operations necessary to neutralise the consequences of such 'currency substitution' will be straightforward. If depositors in (say) Italian banks did want to move all their funds into German banks, and they were not reassured (and hence deterred) by the willingness of the monetary authorities to execute these transactions without limit, then Italian banks would be in trouble. But the Italian government could fill the hole in their balance sheets if it wished to do so. There could of course be a run on the government debt of a country in the euro region – just as New York got into trouble some years ago (and Italy came close in 1989). But that would be a debt crisis, not a currency crisis. Most if not all government debt will be redenominated into euros.[4]

The previous three external shocks should, by all rational calculations, have already terminated EMU. But another shock of the size which Dr Eltis anticipates would still be technically possible to ignore as Professor Portes anticipates, given political will, paper, ink and a printing press. However ill-advised EMU may be it is a near certainty that there will be a European single currency.

Changing American opinion

In the last few years opinion in the United States has begun to shift, and the somewhat simplistic belief that European integration is necessarily always beneficial to the transatlantic partnership, is not held as religiously as before. Economists, business people, professors of business schools are much more critical of the economics of European integration. Political scientists and sociologists still expect the United States of Europe to be similar to the United States of America, a replica which by implication is a form of flattery. Recently there have been a number of highly critical comments in the United States regarding the whole process of European integration which would have been inconceivable just a few years ago. In the *Wall Street Journal Europe* Gerald Frost has reviewed *European Integration and American Interests: What the New Europe Really Means for the United States*, edited by Jeffrey Gedmin and published by the American Enterprise Institute. As Mr Frost observes, some authors continue to argue that a politically integrated Europe would provide a strong second pillar to the alliance. But many others correctly perceive that the new Europe will not imitate the free-trading, free-market habits of the US and that a politically integrated Europe is far less likely to follow US leadership on foreign policy questions than the states from which the new federal entity is being constructed. Others call into question its democratic credentials.

Together with other indicators, such arguments suggest that a major sea change of opinion – perhaps to be followed by changes to policy – many soon be under way. In an article in *The Sunday Times*, Irwin Stelzer noted that :

as Europe opts for policies reducing its competitiveness in world markets, it inevitably drifts towards protectionism. That is how Americans see the European Commission's intervention in the merger of Boeing and McDonnell Douglas. The claim of Karel Van Miert, competition commissioner, that he is intervening only to test the merger's effect on competition is risible. Rather, he is trying to protect Europe's Airbus from the greater competition the merged American company may offer. Any doubts that this is the case were dispelled when Van Miert also decided to challenge the signing by an American airline, Delta, of a long-term contract to buy jets from an American supplier, Boeing. Such protectionist measures are necessary because European labour costs make it difficult for European companies to compete with American ones. And those labour costs are high because Europe wants to maintain a welfare state more generous than America's, which the French deride as acceptable to barbaric Anglo-Saxons but not to their own, more refined, sensibilities. In short, it seems Europe wants to preserve its welfare states and at the same time cut unemployment by closing its markets to American goods.[5]

Similarly, criticism of monetary union is now commonplace. Robert Samuelson of *Newsweek*, writing in *The Washington Post*, commented that:

[The euro] is a lunatic idea, but to be honest, one that I thought would collapse of its own stupidity. Unfortunately, it hasn't, and so here goes. Europe suffers from an obsession with economic security that translates into economic stagnation. It over-regulates industry. High payroll taxes penalise hiring. Even Europeans don't contend that a single currency would cure these ills automatically. The argument is that the requirements establishing the euro would force countries to make reforms that would revitalise their economies. Though seductive, the logic won't wash. If all Europe's countries met these requirements, it's questionable whether their economies would surge. Their problems stem from excessively restrictive taxes, regulations, labour practices and welfare programs that wouldn't necessarily be affected. What can we do? Not much. American officials ought to stop treating the project with a respectful silence and express the skepticism that it deserves. Otherwise, our only hope is that the Europeans will come to their senses. The single currency is an economic version of the Maginot Line, the long string of fortresses that the French thought would prevent World War II. Like the euro, it was a grand delusion.[6]

There are now voices in the United States which are saying exactly what I and other Eurosceptics have been saying for a decade or more. There is a proper debate in the United States about European integration, whether it really is leading to greater transatlantic cooperation, or whether the European project has a quite different objective. This brings me to those five areas where the single currency will adversely affect the possibility of increased transatlantic cooperation.

The effect of EMU on transatlantic cooperation

1. Optimal currency area

Firstly, the European Union is not and shows no sign of becoming an optimal currency area. It is not a replica of the economy in the United States in the way the European Commission constantly claims.[7] In the

United States a common language and a flexible labour market make possible an optimal currency area, but these two crucial and necessary factors are absent from the EMU process. In his brilliant lecture at the London School of Economics, Vaclav Klaus, the Prime Minister of the Czech Republic, made exactly this point.[8] He argued that any traditional economics textbook, in the section on optimal currency areas, will stress microeconomic criteria; yet such microeconomic considerations are absent from the convergence criteria of the Maastricht Treaty.

It is clear that as the European Union gets closer to the single currency the economies within it are diverging not converging. In 1992, Martin Feldstein, Professor of Economics at Harvard and former chairman of the Council of Economic Advisers, writing about European Monetary Union, correctly predicted that 'monetary union is not needed to achieve the advantages of a free trade zone. On the contrary, an artificially contrived monetary union might actually reduce the volume of trade, and would almost certainly increase the level of unemployment.'[9]

Similarly, Professor Milton Friedman has argued that:

> The relevant question is not whether the euro is economically viable – it is if the member states are willing to exercise the necessary discipline, as they did from 1870 to 1914 under the gold standard – but whether it is preferable to flexible exchange rates. Does the gain from greater discipline and lower transaction costs outweigh the loss from dispensing with an effective adjustment mechanism and having to rely entirely on price and wage changes to absorb differential impacts of economic events on the different countries?
>
> My considered opinion has long been that the loss outweighs the gain. The potential members of the EMU do not have sufficiently flexible wages and prices, or sufficiently mobile workers, or a sufficiently effective fiscal compensatory mechanism, to serve as a satisfactory substitute for flexible exchange rates.[10]

This view is echoed by Johns Hopkins economics Professor Steve H. Hawke, who has observed that:

> This grand scheme poses a dilemma. A unified currency area can function well only if markets within it are flexible. But European markets, particularly labor markets, are notoriously inflexible. Setting aside the natural limitations of language and culture, European labor markets suffer from government-imposed rigidities: high minimum wages, confiscatory labor taxes, overgenerous unemployment bene-

fits, national social security entitlements, nonportability of pension rights and public subsidies to ailing industries.

To produce the benefits advertised by the propagandists of the European Monetary Union, member countries would have to embrace US style flexible labor markets. Not a chance. The mere mention of flexible markets constitutes blasphemy in Brussels. Indeed, the Eurocrats claim that Anglo-Saxon deregulation would mean 'a return to Dickensian sweatshops.'[11]

Thus the United States has a deregulated full employment economy in contrast to the EU. The United States has 4.7 per cent unemployed compared to 11 per cent in the EU. And American growth rates have outperformed the EU for the last 21 years. The obvious conclusion is that the European Union is not an optimal currency area, and is not becoming an economic replica of the United States. A single currency under the current plans would lead to divergence between the European and the American economies which would retard genuine cooperation.

Workable on the continent?

But to what extent will the single currency work for the continentals? There are those who argue that it is quite possible for a single currency to work in a geographical area as large as the European continent because a single currency works well over the large geographical area that is the United States of America. The European Commission on many occasions has argued that the American economy has a single currency and therefore the European economy should have a single currency. It has even suggested satirically that if America wanted to have the same arrangements as Europe then it would need to create fifty different currencies. Without any doubt the United States works well as an optimal currency area. It has a single monetary policy and an independent bank, the Federal Reserve, which historically has worked well to guarantee currency stability. But any deeper consideration of the economic details shows that the EC Commission's analogy breaks down.

The American economy works well as an optimal currency area because there is freedom of movement resulting from a flexible labour market so that any external shocks to parts of the American economy can be absorbed by workers moving from one state to another. This process occurred in the United States in the mid-1980s, for example, when the rust-bowl smokestack depression of the Northeast led to a considerable migration of workers to the booming South and south-western computer- and technology-based Sunbelt states.

Moreover, this process of flexible labour mobility is greatly facilitated by a common language. A third factor which enables the Americans to have a successful optimal currency area is that the tax regime is also flexible. Effectively there are 51 tax regimes, with the federal tax regime supplementing each state's own individualistic tax regime. Each of the 50 states works out its tax regime to suit its own interests. Some states such as Texas have no income tax, whereas New York has the reverse. Iowa has a gambling tax in contrast to neighbouring Nebraska. While monetary policy is rigid, fiscal policy is very flexible and adaptable to local needs and democratic decisions.

In continental Europe none of these three criteria apply. On the contrary, there is a sclerotic and rigid labour market dominated, in the worst instances, by Scargill-style trade unions which prevent any meaningful relationship between the supply and demand for labour. Nor is there a common European language. It is very difficult for workers to move even within countries, as the problems between north and south Italy and German unification prove. Labour mobility is inhibited within countries let alone between them. Additionally, over the last decade, Europe has embraced a rigid and inflexible tax structure based on a minimum-level Valued Added Tax across the whole continent at 15 per cent. This politically inspired rigidity is the very opposite approach to fiscal policy to that pursued by the Americans. For all these reasons the European economy is not analogous to the American economy.

If a single European currency is imposed on divergent economies, a single interest rate will produce either circumstances of uncontrolled inflation or circumstances of depression, low growth and high unemployment in different regions. If the exchange rate cannot take the strain (in the absence of exchange rates) then the strain will be taken by growth and employment, condemning areas of the EU to a near-permanent recession. The damaging consequences of such an outcome are profound and long-term. As the Bradford University research has graphically illustrated, under EMU:

> Long before structural changes may be encouraged by the operation of market forces, any sizeable asymmetric shock would undermine an EMU project, unable to resolve the fundamental problem of how a single, federal monetary authority can design and implement a single economic programme which can respond to changes in the external economic environment affecting individual nations in markedly different ways. Therefore, the persistence of asymmetric shocks would continually undermine the efforts of the federal EU authorities to

reduce unemployment and income inequalities, which will therefore increasingly diverge across the EMU zone. The inability of a single currency, on its present basis, to solve this problem will foster disillusionment with the European integration project until it begins to unravel with devastating consequences.[12]

In these circumstances, however, there would be no prospect of liberation similar to that which enabled Britain to escape from the ERM on White Wednesday in September 1992. This argument has been made as often as it has been ignored by the EU. Professor Wilhelm Nölling of Hamburg University, a former Bundesbank Council member (1982–92), argues that 'Europe's most pressing challenge is combating mass unemployment. Yet monetary union would impose a costly straitjacket that would make a bad situation worse. Fixing exchange rates will remove states' ability to make corrections needed to economic policies by changing the exchange rate. Instead of such flexibility the rigidities of monetary union would lead to more unemployment.'[13] Moreover, as Professor Anthony Thirlwall has cogently argued,[14] the stability pact fines for countries whose budget deficits exceed 3 per cent of GDP – agreed at the 1996 Dublin summit – make no distinction between structural and cyclical deficits. In a recessionary shock, therefore, fines of up to 0.2 per cent of GDP would compound both the recession and the deficit.

Similarly Eddie George, Governor of the Bank of England, has stated that:

> the Euro member countries will have no possibility to adjust either interest rates or the exchange rate independently and they will have somewhat limited scope for independent fiscal adjustment. So the risk is that a 'one size fits all' interest rate could result in economic weakness and unemployment in some areas, if the central bank pursued a firm monetary policy, or unwanted inflation in others if it were more accommodating. Without genuinely sustainable convergence – I emphasised the word sustainable – serious tensions could emerge between different countries living with a single monetary policy.[15]

The Governor of the Bank of England is absolutely right to conclude that, in effect, the EU is not an optimal currency area.

Workable for Britain? – ten UK objections

If the single currency is ill-advised for the continent, it is even less suited for the United Kingdom, whose economy is structurally and fundamentally different from the continental economies. Britain needs to retain the ability to set its own interest rates, and to maintain full control over taxation and fiscal policy. The best relationship that Britain can have with the continental economies is free trade. Alas a free trade area, unencumbered with political union, has proved elusive both before and after British EEC membership in 1973. The truth remains that the UK economy is fundamentally different from the continental economies for the following ten reasons which ought to necessitate the indefinite maintenance of the pound and an indefinite rejection of the single currency.

1   The UK business cycle is nearly always out of line with the continental business cycle. In May 1999, UK interest rates at 5.25 per cent contrasted with 2.75 per cent in the euro countries. For 20 years or more the British business cycle has become less, not more, aligned with that of other EU nations.[16]

2   Britain has a different trade and investment pattern from the continentals. We are globalists with a profound interest in worldwide trade. Only the Germans have anything remotely similar to our global trade profile among the EU members. Britain has a balance of payments surplus with every continent on the planet except Europe. In 1996 there was a surplus of £9 billion with the rest of the world but a deficit of £12 billion with the European Union. Over the previous 23 years since Britain joined the EEC, the accumulative balance of payments deficit with the European Union was £151 billion compared to a surplus with the rest of the world of £70 billion. Profound differences in trading patterns between Britain and the EU are likely to grow as the UK welcomes the globalisation which Europe fears.

3   The pound often moves on the foreign exchange markets in line with the dollar rather than with any continental currency, which reflects the similarities in both economic interests and economic philosophy between Britain and the United States. Both nations prefer free trade, free markets, and the global approach to economics based on Anglo-Saxon economic thought, originating with Adam Smith and David Ricardo. The mercantilist philosophy still dominates the economic thinking on the continent as the promotion of the European 'Social Model' indicates.

4   The UK housing market is totally different from the continental housing market because of variable mortgage interest rates and because housing costs form a far greater proportion of household

expenditure. Mortgage payments in the UK are on average 10.9 per cent of income compared to 3.5 per cent on the continent. Britain should never permit interest rates, which affect every mortgage, to be set by an unaccountable European Central Bank.

5 Britain has lower taxes as a per portion GDP (35 per cent) compared with the continental average (42 per cent).[17] Tax harmonisation will push up British levels to the continental level, taking us back close to the penal tax policies which predated the Thatcher government in 1979. Moreover European governments' spending now accounts for 49.5 per cent of GDP compared to 37 per cent in 1970, while current US government spending accounts for only 32 per cent of GDP having risen only 2 per cent in 15 years.[18] The implication of EU policy has been clearly stated by both Yves-Thibault de Silguy, the EMU Commissioner, and by Mario Monti, the Tax Commissioner, who have called for tax 'harmonisation' to 'prohibit fiscal dumping'.[19] Such a policy would penalise Britain and would remove one of the most important incentives to the burgeoning foreign direct investment in the UK. No wonder that even John Major – albeit since leaving office – has castigated the tax-harmonisation folly.[20]

6 The funding of pensions is totally different in the United Kingdom compared to that on the continent, being much more soundly based as a contributory system with less potential debt overhang. Indeed the House of Commons Social Security Select Committee argued that in a single currency British taxpayers could end up paying at least partially for the pension liabilities of the continentals.

7 Britain has a flexible labour market as a result of 1980s Thatcherite reforms compared to the inflexible labour market which is such a marked feature in Europe. Under a single currency it would only be a matter of time before the UK would be forced to adopt the continental labour practices, as part of the harmonisation process of economic and monetary union.[21]

8 Britain has found it very difficult to digest some of the existing common policies of the European Union such as the Common Agricultural Policy (CAP), the common fisheries policy, and the budgetary policy whereby the UK is a net contributor year after year. Severe structural differences between the British and the European economies lie at the heart of these difficulties. British agriculture, for example, constitutes a much smaller sector in relation to the rest of the economy than on the continent. Not surprisingly successive British governments have, in vain, urged 'reform' of the CAP but British interests would be even better served not by reabsorbing

the CAP but by disgorging it. The deficiencies of the CAP are well documented and government justification of its consequences amounts to little more than a pitiful exercise in damage limitation. If digesting these policies is difficult enough a single monetary policy would be even more indigestible.

9 Britain has a far greater level of privatisation and deregulation than on the continent as a result of the privatisation policy of the Thatcher and Major governments. No equivalent policies have been pursued in Europe outside the new democratic market economics of Central and Eastern Europe.

10 The pound is a petro-currency unlike any continental currency. The value of the pound can be profoundly affected by an oil crisis in the opposite direction to the continental currencies.

For all these reasons the UK economy is complementary to, and dissimilar from, the continental economies.[22] The UK needs free trade with its European neighbours but must retain control of its own economy, maintain its own currency, set its own interest rates, and ultimately safeguard its own democracy.[23] The similarities between the UK and American economies vividly contrast with the structural differences between the UK economy and continental Europe. As these factors become better appreciated on both sides of the Atlantic, initial enthusiasm for EMU will decline. In short it is not in America's interest for the UK to join a monetary union which is not an optimal currency area, as the damage to the UK economy would eventually also damage the United States economy.

2. Different tax regimes

The tax regime in the European Union is totally different from the tax regime in the United States and the single European currency will exacerbate this difference. The key component of the tax regime of the European Union is Valued Added Tax (VAT) which is levied at a minimum rate of 15 per cent across all 15 countries irrespective of their economic circumstances. There is no equivalent of this rigidity in the United States and nor indeed in Asia-Pacific. A federal indirect tax of 15 per cent is not on the agenda in the United States. Europe has long planned for tax harmonisation, with a tax commissioner, whose task it is to harmonise taxes. But the great success story of the American economy is that there is no tax harmonisation; instead there are 51 different tax regimes. Tax competition helps the market economy and is the opposite to what the Europeans are initiating. If the VAT regime becomes ever more severe, if it is followed by harmonisation of direct taxes and property taxes, it will exacerbate the differences between the European economy and the North American economy, making more difficult genuine transatlantic cooperation.

The big problem with VAT is that it is a tax on the factors of production. Any tax on the factors of production reduces production and output. VAT is a great way of raising revenue, but at the expense of reducing economic growth. VAT is acceptable for the multinational large companies which employ many accountants anyway, but it is a vicious and crushing burden on the small and medium-size business sector. This is one of the reasons why small business flourishes in North America but is stunted and retarded in Europe. The House of Commons Select Committee Report on VAT in 1994 'painted a nightmarish picture of businessmen ensnared in a web of rules and regulations so complex that only a minority pay their full VAT dues. Members of Parliament noted with concern that VAT is governed by 156 main regulations, and that there have been 209 regulatory changes in the last nine years.'[24]

A single European currency will simply intensify this process at the expense of genuine transatlantic cooperation. Most recently American opinion has become especially sceptical about this aspect of European monetary union. Nobel economics laureate James M. Buchanan has argued that

> efforts to regularise or harmonise fiscal and regulatory controls (including taxes) across all of Europe are similar to all cartel-like proposals. They are designed to stifle competition at the expense of citizens. Competition among units will itself generate pressures toward uniformities in tax and regulatory structures. But enforced uniformities prior to the working out of competition remove all potential advantages of federalised structures.[25]

Fellow Nobel laureate Milton Friedman concurs, forcefully pointing out that

> The key need for the single market is to avoid the use of taxes as a surrogate for barriers to trade – that is, as concealed subsidies or duties. Beyond that, competition, not identity, among countries in government taxation and spending is highly desirable. How can competition be good in the provision of private goods and services but bad in the provision of governmental goods and services? A government tax and spending cartel is as objectionable as a private cartel.[26]

Professor Arthur Lafter has also criticised tax harmonisation as follows:

> The biggest regional monopolies in Europe are the overbearing governments using the rule of law to exact huge sums from their unwitting citizenries. Goodness knows the last thing Europeans need is a transnational legal structure allowing their bloated governments to collude in setting tax rates. Tax harmonisation is the English-language euphemism for collusion. No matter how warm and fuzzy it sounds, tax harmonisation is the single biggest threat Europeans face in their quest for lasting prosperity. If they aren't allowed to vote on taxes directly, people do vote for the governments of their choice with their feet. Tax harmonisation takes away that choice. It should come as no surprise that there is total unanimity among the governments of Europe that tax harmonisation is a good thing. It's their way to protect their monopoly on the power to tax.[27]

Similarly Professor Robert Mundell of Columbia University has argued that

> If countries with efficient tax structures were required to adopt the taxes of their less efficiently taxed partners, the area as a whole would be worse off. Tax reform is beneficial only if the tax structures of most of the countries are changed for the better. The issue is not so much that countries should have the same tax system as that they should have an efficient tax system. No one should argue that a country with very low tariffs and taxes would be better off adopting the high tariffs and taxes of its neighbors.[28]

3. Trade policy

The big difference between Europe and the United States over trade policy is not a question of political-pressure lobbying to procure pork-barrel protectionism. The difference is ideological because in North America, at least since the Smoot Hawley tariff fiasco of the 1930s, trade policy has ceased to be ideological in a way that it has always been in Europe. The European Union uses trade policy as an ideological tool to foster European integration. The pursuit of a European identity is what Airbus is all about. Europeanism has become an ideology to which trade policy is subordinated. What the Europeans like about the Common Agricultural Policy is not so much the agriculture but the fact that it is *common*; it is a building block for integration which is not amenable to rationality. It is impossible to have an intelligent debate on trade in the

European Union because ideology gets in the way. EU ideology advocates the customs union model which is a twentieth century version of the mercantilist approach of the seventeenth century. That is why the CAP will never be reformed, that is why the European Union is so protectionist with regard to textiles, damaging Third World countries, particularly in the Indian sub-continent. It is why the outdated European Coal and Steel Community is totally unreformable.[29] For these reasons, I think that North America will continue down the path of liberalising markets, which other distinguished contributors have described; but that the European Union will stay essentially autarchic. The North American Free Trade Area (NAFTA), as George Bush, Margaret Thatcher and more recently Newt Gingrich and Conrad Black have advocated, ought to develop as the Transatlantic Free Trade Area (TAFTA). Tragically it is the European Union which keeps this off the agenda.

4.   Interest rates and exchange rates

There is fundamental difference between the United States and the European Union in interest rate and exchange rate policy. In the United States, Alan Greenspan does not follow the dogma of exchange rate monetarism. By and large, the Federal Reserve sets interest rates to suit the domestic monetary circumstances in the United States to sensibly balance inflation and unemployment. Thus President Clinton's speech in Colorado[30] rightly praised Alan Greenspan's approach. By contrast the continentals have failed in Europe by pursuing exchange-rate targeting and exchange-rate monetarism. During the recession in the early 1990s, when the rest of the world cut their interest rates, interest rates in Europe rose sharply. Not surprisingly, Europe's rate of growth has been much lower and the rate of unemployment much higher than in North America. There is a fundamental difference in interest-rates policy and exchange-rate policy which weakens the transatlantic partnership. A single European currency would make this worse. It would very soon be a political virility symbol for those who believe that a strong currency creates a strong economy. But any reputable economist will argue that the truth is the other way round; a strong currency is the consequence of a strong economy.

5.   Foreign direct investment

During the world investment boom over the last decade, the European Union has been losing out to North America, to the Asian-Pacific countries, and to Eastern Europeans. For example, 32 per cent of the Czech Republic economy is now comprised of FDI. Forty per cent of all

American and Japanese investment in the EU is in Britain. Compared to other parts of the world, Europe has underperformed because of its rigid labour market, its high tax regime, over-regulation and harmonisation. The EU has lost out in terms of this great global investment boom. The OECD 1995 report argued that the EU economies have been losing out to the US in the competition for foreign direct investment. Inflows of foreign direct investment to the US economy nearly tripled to $60.07 billion in 1994 from $21.37 billion in 1993. The 1994 figure also marked a sixfold increase from the $9.89 billion of such investment into the US in 1992. The totals underscore perceptions that the US has emerged as a favoured destination among OECD economies for multinational companies because of its big market and its competitive base. In Europe, Italy saw foreign-investment inflows slow to 34 per cent, while French inflows slipped 13 per cent and the UK slipped 24 per cent. Once again there is divergence between the European Union economies and North America, which a single currency would only worsen.

Conclusion

In conclusion, what we are seeing now is a clash between two quite different economic experiments. The Anglo-Saxon free market model is being pursued by North America and, to a lesser extent, by the rest of the world, but not by the European Union. The EU's mercantilist middle way is the 'Rhineland' version of capitalism to which former Prime Minister John Major referred during the 1997 election campaign. The European Union's economic philosophy is different from that of North America in that economic philosophy in Europe is intertwined with the political project to create a European superstate.

This is no less than a new ideology. It is driven by the desire to have a European identity for just about everything, economic and political. Such Europeanism is hostile towards globalism. The North American model works well with the grain of globalism, as Bill Clinton's Colorado speech indicated; but I cannot remember a single European Union leader making that kind of speech because the Europeans see globalism not as a welcome challenge, but as an unwelcome distraction. The single European currency will make these differences worse.

I am not arguing that the continentals should change their approach; that would be arrogant and would fail to understand the reasons why they have embarked on their project. But what I do urge is that it is about time that we now started recognising that these differences are for real. The American and EU economies are not converging and the differences are not going to go away. We have to confront the reality that European integration is damaging the process of transatlantic partnership. Enough evidence indicates that the Eurosceptics have won this argument and now occupy the intellectual high ground. We need to understand that the United States and the European Union are moving in fundamentally different directions, and the quicker we understand that, the better equipped we will be to address a central question affecting the future of the Atlantic Community.

Notes

1 Dean Acheson, *Present at the Creation* (New York: Signet, 1970), p. 446.
2 Norman Lamont, Bruges Group Press Release, 25 March 1998.
3 Walter Eltis, *The Creation and Destruction of EMU* (London: Centre for Policy Studies, 1997).
4 Richard Portes, *The Risk of a Currency Crisis in EMU* (London: CEPR, 1998). See also Wolfgang Münchau, 'Speculation perils persist at endgame', *Financial Times*, 24 February 1998.
5 *Sunday Times*, 8 June 1997.
6 *Washington Post*, 8 January 1997.
7 See, for example, the 1989 Delors Report on Economic and Monetary Union.
8 Speech delivered at the London School of Economics, 17 June 1997.
9 Article in *The Economist*, 13 June 1992.
10 Article in the *Wall Street Journal Europe*, 23 June 1997.
11 Ibid.
12 See B. Burkitt, M. Baimbridge, and P. Whyman, *A Price Not Worth Paying* (CIB, London, 1997).
13 Wilhelm Nölling, *The European Journal*, May 1996.
14 See Professor Anthony Thirlwall, 'The Folly of the Euro', *The European Journal*, March 1998.
15 Speech in Hong Kong, 23 September 1997.
16 For an excellent analysis of this point see Daniel Hannan, *Eurofacts*, 7 November 1997.
17 *The Times*, 16 April 1998, reported that French companies and businesses are registering in Britain to reduce their tax liabilities, to the outrage and consternation of the French government.
18 See David Roche, 'EMU needs a new social contract', the *Wall Street Journal Europe*, 6 April 1998; and 'Letter from America', *The Times*, 21 April 1998.
19 See *The European Journal*, January 1998, p. 21.
20 John Major, in *The Daily Telegraph*, 15 April 1998.
21 For a discussion of this prospect see John Grahl, *After Maastricht: a Guide to European Monetary Union* (London: Lawrence & Wishart, 1998).

22 For a further discussion of this theme, see M. Baimbridge, B. Burkitt and P. Whyman, *Is Europe Ready for EMU?: Theory Evidence and Consequences*, Bruges Group Occasional Paper No. 31, London, 1998.
23 For an extensive examination of these points see M. Holmes, ed., *The Eurosceptical Reader* (London: Macmillan, 1996).
24 HMSO publication 1994, reported in *The Times*, 5 August 1994. For a further discussion of this theme, see M. Holmes, *From Single Market to Single Currency: Evaluating Europe's Economic Experiment*, Bruges Group publication, London, 1995.
25 *Wall Street Journal Europe*, 29 July 1998.
26 Ibid.
27 Ibid.
28 Ibid.
29 See I. Stelzer, 'Euro trade barriers fire up protectionists', *The Sunday Times*, 3 August 1997.
30 Speech in Colorado by President Clinton, 19 June 1997.

Index

Adenauer, Konrad 10n., 133
Africa 33, 60, 62, 72
Airborne Warning and Control Systems
  (AWACS) 50, 63
Albania 23–4, 36, 53
Albright, Madeleine 21, 82–3
Algeria 76
America see United States of America
Argentina 109
Asia-Pacific Economic Cooperation
  forum (APEC) 114
Atlantic Council of the United
  Kingdom xiii
Austria 25–7, 37

Ballistic Missiles and Anti-Missile
  Defence 5, 78–81
  Anti-Ballistic Missiles (ABM)
    Technology 64–5, 75
  ABM Treaty 75
  Global Protection against nuclear
    attack (GPALS) 79
  Missile threats 9, 38, 74
Baltic States 20, 22, 27
Baylor University xi
Blair, Tony (British Prime
  Minister) 82, 91
Boeing-McDonnell Douglas
  merger 94, 129, 138
Bosnia 8–9, 19, 39
Brazil 106–7, 111
Britain (United Kingdom or
  UK) viii–x, 5, 6, 14, 25, 30, 32, 40,
  45, 82–4, 86, 88, 126, 133
  and the European single currency
  127, 143–6
Bulgaria 7, 20–2, 24, 36
Bush, President George 17, 109, 149

Canada 82–3, 94, 101, 103, 109–10

Central and Eastern Europe 13–29,
  57, 66–8, 73, 97–8, 118, 125–9
Centre for Study of International
  Affairs (Europe and
  America) xi–xiii
Chechnya 28, 69
Chile 109
China 9, 34, 72, 74, 80–1, 99
Chirac, President Jacques 6, 123
Clinton, President William 54, 82,
  84, 150
Clinton Administration 18–19, 68,
  82, 105
Cold War viii, xii, 1–10, 15, 25–6, 29,
  30–2, 34, 38, 41, 43, 53, 62, 65, 71,
  77, 80, 84
Collective Security and Collective
  Defence as concepts 37–9
colonialism 30–1
Combined Joint Task Forces (CJTF) vi,
  40, 46–54, 75, 88, 90–1
Common Foreign and Security Policy
  (CFSP) see European Union
Commonwealth of Independent States
  (CIS) 32, 44, 72–3
Connolly, Bernard 123, 131n.
Conventional Forces in Europe (CFE)
  Treaty 73, 75
Cook, Robin 82, 84
Croatia 36
Cuba 38
Cyprus 27, 100
Czech Republic viii, 3, 4, 13, 15–17,
  36, 68, 84, 118, 127, 149

defence technology 4–6, 60–2, 66, 68
  Alliance ground technology
    (AGS) 63–4
  Joint surveillance and targeting
    systems (JSTARS) 63–4

defence technology (*cont.*)
  Theatre missile defence (TMD)   65
Dedman, Martin   xiv, 117
Denmark   125

economic and industrial
  revolution   35–6
Eden, Douglas   xiv, 1
Eltis, Dr Walter   136–7
Estonia   36
European Defence Community (EDC)
  (1950–54)   119
European Economic and Monetary
  Union (EMU)   vii, 45, 117–31,
  132–52
  Euro (single currency)   x, 120–4,
    137–9
  Tax harmonisation   146–8, 150
  US opinion 137–41
  See also Maastricht Treaty *under*
    European Union (EU)
European Security and Defence
  Identity (ESDI)   vi, ix, xi, 6, 7, 40,
  44, 47, 51, 90
European Union (EU) vi, xi, 3, 6, 7, 9,
  15, 16, 18, 21, 32, 33, 43–4, 45, 57,
  65, 68, 73, 81, 83, 94, 96, 109, 114,
  117–31, 132–52
  Common Agriculture Policy
    (CAP)   97–8, 118, 145–6, 148
  Common Defence and Security
    Policy (CDSP)   6
  Common Foreign and Security Policy
    (CFSP)   vi, ix, xiii, 41, 73, 125
  Competition Policy   137–9
  enlargement   7, 71, 92, 117–18, 122,
    124–8
  Maastricht Treaty on European
    Union (1992)   40–1, 117,
    119–22, 134–7
  Madrid Summit with USA (1995)   8
  Value Added Tax (VAT)   142, 146–7

Finland   25–7, 37
France   ix–x, 5–6, 22, 25, 28, 30, 51,
  73–4, 122

General Agreement on Tariffs and
  Trade (GATT)   101

Germany   vii–x, 4–6, 10–11, 15–17,
  25, 28, 30, 32, 40–1, 45, 59, 74,
  133
Gorbachev, Mikhail   17
Greece   13, 17
Greenspan, Alan   149
Gulf War (Operation Desert
  Storm, 1991)   39, 58, 60, 63,
  69, 76

Holmes, Martin   xiv, 132
Hungary   vii, 13, 15–17, 26, 28, 36, 68,
  85, 100, 118, 127
Hurd, Douglas   125

India   5, 74
Information Technology
  Agreement   96
Iran   64, 76, 78
Iraq   xi, 66, 76, 78
Irish Republic   37, 125
Ismay, General Lord   2, 10
Israel   101
Italy   22, 28, 30, 122–3

Japan   30, 32, 34, 64, 72

Kissinger, Henry   19, 126, 133
Kohl, Helmut   41, 120, 123, 127–8
Kosovo and K-For   ix, xi, 7–9, 23,
  72

Latvia   36
Lawson, Nigel   124
The Levant   58
Libya   64
Lott, Trent   82
Luxembourg   135

McKinney, Joseph A.   xiv, 101
Macedonia   7, 23, 36
Mader, William   xv, 13
Major, John   132, 145, 150
Marshall Plan   3
Mexico   95, 101–3
Milosevic, Slobodan   vii, viii
missile threats *see* ballistic missiles
Mitterrand, President
  François   123

nationalism 72
NATO (North Atlantic Treaty
    Organisation) 1–10, 13–29,
    30, 32–54, 58–9, 63, 64–9,
    71–5, 78–80, 84, 91–2, 114, 117,
    132
  Article 5 of the Washington
    Treaty 19, 40, 46, 118
  Euro-Atlantic Partnership Council
    (EAPC) (formerly North Atlantic
    Cooperation Council) 22, 40,
    44, 72, 86
  enlargement 2–29, 36–40, 57–70,
    71, 83, 88, 92, 113, 117–18,
    124–9
  Madrid Summit (1997) 13, 22, 82,
    85, 88–90
  mission and military doctrine 2–10
  Operation Allied Force vii, 8
  Partnership for Peace (PFP) vi, 21,
    40, 72, 75, 86–8
  'Strategic Concept' (or 'New Strategic
    Concept') vi, viii, 8, 78
  Washington Summit Conference
    (1999) 8, 78
New Labour xi, 82, 83
Newquist, Don E. xvii, 92
New Trans-Atlantic Agenda
    (NTAA) 99, 118, 125, 129
North American Free Trade Agreement
    (NAFTA) vii, 93–4, 98–9, 101–3,
    109–10, 129, 149
North Korea 64, 76, 78
nuclear weapons *see* weapons of mass
    destruction

Organisation for Economic
    Cooperation and Development
    (OECD) 96
Organisation for Security and
    Cooperation in Europe
    (OSCE) 27, 32, 47

Pakistan 5, 74, 78
Partnership for Peace (PFP) *see* NATO
Poland vii, 13, 15–17, 25, 36, 66, 85,
    118, 125, 127–9
Portes, Richard 137
Portugal 85

Priestley, P.J. xi, xv, 82
Primakov, Yevgeny 17

Rifkind, Malcolm 125
Romania 7, 16, 20–4, 28, 36
Russia 16, 17, 40–1, 44–5, 67, 73, 86,
    99, 127
  NATO–Russia Founding Act on
    Mutual Relations, Cooperation
    and Security (1997) 18, 73,
    85–6, 88, 91, 126
  NATO–Russian Permanent Joint
    Council (PJC) 73, 129

Schneider, William, Jr xi, xv, 57
Schröder, Gerhard 123
Second World War 30, 34–5, 47
Slovenia 15–16, 20–2, 27, 29, 36
Solana, Javier 11n., 42
Soviet Union 1, 3, 7, 13, 30, 35, 38,
    59–60, 74, 77
Spain 13, 122
Strategic Arms Limitation Treaties
    (START I and II) 73, 75, 77
Sweden 25–7, 37

Technology and technological
    revolution 34–6, 61
Thatcher, Margaret 124, 132
trade (transatlantic)
  Mutual Recognition Agreements
    (MRAs) 95–6
  New Transatlantic Marketplace
    (NTM) 9, 118, 129
  Transatlantic Business Dialogue
    (TABD) 95, 99
  Transatlantic Economic
    Partnership 114
  Transatlantic Free Trade Area
    (TAFTA) 9, 36
  US–EU trade vii, 92–3, 148–51
  US–Latin American trade
    implications 108–9
Turkey 13, 27

Ukraine 15, 19–20
United Kingdom *see* Britain
United Nations 31–2, 37, 76, 77,
    79

156 *Index*

United States of America 14, 25, 28,
    30, 32, 35, 37–8, 41, 51, 57–69, 72,
    74, 76, 80–3, 88, 101–2, 106, 110,
    112, 125
  and European Monetary
    Union 117–30, 137–9
  Quadrennial Defence Review (QDR)
    1997 60–2
  Interests in Europe 3–5, 58–60, 62–3,
    92–100, 132–4
  US Congress 69, 82, 103, 112

Warsaw Pact 13–14
Weapons of Mass Destruction
    (WMD) ix, 71, 74, 77, 80
  proliferation and non-
    proliferation 5, 9, 64, 75–9
  Comprehensive Test Ban
    Treaty 75
Weimar Republic 3
West Germany 119–20, 125–7

Western European Union
    (WEU) 39–42, 47–53, 59, 125
Western Hemisphere 101–2, 104,
    110–11, 113
  Latin American and US trade 108–9
  MERCOSUR 109–10
  Organisation of American States
    (OAS) 106–7
  Summit of the Americas (1994)
    104–8
  See also North American Free Trade
    Agreement (NAFTA)
Williams, Alan Lee xi, xvi, 71
Williams, Geoffrey Lee xi, xvi, 30
World Trade Organisation (WTO) x,
    93, 95, 97–9, 104, 112
World War II *see* Second World War

Yalta Conference (1945) 14
Yeltsin, President Boris 67, 69, 85, 125
Yugoslavia vii, 5, 8, 83